To Sean,
Keep shining
your Light.
♡ Heidi

Step into YOUR Spotlight

Inspiring Women to Play Bigger!

Heidi Parr Kerner, M.A.

Aurora Corialis Publishing

Pittsburgh, PA

Step into Your Spotlight: Inspiring Women to Play Bigger!

For more information, please email the publisher cori@coriwamsley.com.

Hardcover ISBN: 978-1-958481-89-9

Ebook ISBN: 978-1-958481-91-2

Printed in the United States of America

Cover by Karen Captline, BetterBe Creative

Developmental Editing by Brianna Lyle, Lyle Editorial

Edited by Allison Hrip, Aurora Corialis Publishing

Cover photos and headshots of Heidi by Paul Lorei Studios

Praise

"If your dreams don't scare you, they are not BIG enough. Heidi Parr Kerner's book *Step into YOUR Spotlight* is the perfect "Script for Success" introducing Confidence, Charisma and Courage into any role you may be playing... personally or professionally. It's time to be the leading lady of your own life!"

~ Barbara Niven

Actress, Producer, Speaker, and Bestselling Author of *111 Star Power Tips: Insider Secrets from a Hollywood Pro*

"To play bigger and create wealth and abundance in all areas of your life, you must start with a clear vision and have the confidence to 'own' what you truly want.

"In *Step into your Spotlight*, Heidi shares how to believe in yourself and how important it is to get out of your comfort zone and ask for help.

"This book is truly an invitation for women to trust their inner wisdom and be courageous in the pursuit of their dreams!"

~ Susan Wilson Solovic

Author of *The Girls' Guide to Power and Success* and *The Girls' Guide to Building a Million Dollar Business*

"Powerhouse advice from a super star!

"A little sass, a little sparkle, and a whole lot of charisma, Heidi Parr Kerner's *Step into Your Spotlight* tells it like it is for any shy misfits longing for action and playing bigger.

"Changing schools often with her family's travels, she was one of the shy ones who feared new schools and trying to fit in. But she persevered, learning how to find her power and make her own way. Now, in this book, she gives *you* the roadmap so you can find your own confidence, courage, and charisma. This is a must-read guide for all who want to shine in their own spotlight. Heidi shows you just how to transform yourself into the star of your life that you deserve to be!"

~ Chellie Campbell

Author of *The Wealthy Spirit* and *From Worry to Wealthy*

"I am so glad that I had the opportunity to read *Step into Your Spotlight* by Heidi Parr Kerner. She authentically takes us on her journey from being a shy young girl to leaning on her inner game tools that she refers to as "Sisters" and blooms into a beautiful and brilliant woman. She put her journey into action by being of service and works with other women to step into their spotlight. I highly recommend this book."

~Joie Gharrity

Brand Consultant, Podcaster, International Speaker, Author of *Being Your Own Superstar* and *The Red Carpet Guide to Visibility and Influence*

"Wow! I loved reading Heidi Parr Kerner's book *Step into Your Spotlight*, which is filled with her years of wisdom and experience. It offers the steps to guide you to manifest your dreams in business and in your personal life.

"I had the honor to meet Heidi, "The Networking Queen," in the late 1980s at a big L.A. networking event she was leading. We had an instant connection, and I was blessed to become part of a "Goddess" mastermind group with her and other amazing, busy wonder women. We gathered monthly for many years and supported each other on our paths to success in our businesses and personal lives. This group's support helped us all manifest our dreams!

"This amazing book is filled with her years of experience, wisdom, and the steps to guide you to manifest more success in all areas of your life. Her inspiring stories and tips will ignite you to forge ahead to achieve your goals… and to shine your light while you're doing it!"

~Renée Piane ~ The Love Designer

Author of *Love Mechanics: The Power Tools to Build Successful Relationships with Women, Get Real about LOVE: The Secrets to Opening your Heart & Finding True Love*, and *The Art of Flirting with Life: Making Great Connections for Love, Friendship & Business*

"I really enjoyed reading *Step into Your Spotlight*! Heidi is so open and caring in her message of courage, charisma, and confidence to help you reach your goals.

"Less than four years ago, I was a people-pleasing, struggling solopreneur who often struggled with imposter syndrome and self-doubt. I would have loved a copy of Heidi's book at that time to help me come into my true self and step into my personal spotlight faster.

"You will love hearing about Heidi's journey and how she overcame her challenges by embracing the 'three sisters' so you can reach your dream life too! I couldn't put it down!"

~ Alex Pursglove

CEO, Business & Success Coach, Alex Pursglove Coaching | www.alexpursglove.com

---

"I have known Heidi almost as long as I've known my husband, her brother. I have seen her grow into a local celebrity in her hometown Erie, helping dozens of other women find their voice. Now, she is sharing her wisdom with all of us, reminding us to wake up to what our souls are trying to tell us and giving us the tools—confidence, charisma, and courage—to achieve our goals. I would not be the award-winning filmmaker I am today without those tools. I encourage you to step into your own spotlight. This book will show you how."

~ Luchina Fisher

Award-Winning Director, Writer, and Producer

"*Step into Your Spotlight* gives a real, raw look at the challenges that come up in women's lives and how we need to call on our courage, charisma, and confidence to play full out. I love Heidi's honesty about her childhood and career as so many women have been through challenges with shyness and self-discovery versus who they desire to be and how they can find a career that suits them.

"Change can be scary, and Heidi beautifully shows how we can not only navigate it with grace but seek it out and succeed. She covers a lot of her back story, so you get to dive deep into how she became the strong leader she is today. As a coach and speaker myself, her story resonated so much with me. I recommend *Step into Your Spotlight* for any woman who wants to be the star of her own life and get exactly what she wants."

~ Stacy Raske

The InFLOWential™ Activator, Authenticity Alchemist, Leadership Mentor, Mindset Coach, Keynote Speaker, Bestselling Author of *Be a Boss & Fire that Bitch: Quiet Your Inner Critic & Finally Believe You're GOOD ENOUGH*

"This is a gem of a book! It is like getting a decade of coaching with all the tough love you would expect from your best girlfriend in a quick and easy read.

"Heidi and I have worked together for over ten years, and she has coached me as a professional speaker, polished me for TV appearances, and acted as a life coach and mentor to me. So many of Heidi's 'golden nuggets' are here for you to learn from and make yours. Her advice is practical, her writing is personal, and her desire to serve, inspire and uplift women is palpable. A must for any woman looking to shine bright!"

~Stacy Garcia

CEO & Chief Inspiration Officer at Stacy Garcia Inc., a leading design company with global lifestyle brands that add a well-traveled edge to the ever-evolving world of interiors

To my mother, Audrée,

Your grace, wisdom, and support mean more to me than you'll ever know.

Thank you for being an amazing example of what a strong woman truly is and supporting me to step into my own spotlight.

I love you.

~ Heidi

Table of Contents

Foreword
By Phil Kerner

Dear Reader,

Almost two decades ago, I happened to run into a lovely woman at a pre-high school reunion party at a local pub. I noticed her immediately: striking figure, beautiful smile, attractive hairstyle, fashionably dressed.

But my one very vivid memory was how she presented herself: Tall in stature, direct eye contact, comfortable with herself and others. I would learn much later that her manner of presenting herself was a reflection of confidence. Of course at that time, I knew none of that. To summarize my initial impression: "Me likey."

And so the journey began: the blue collar tool and die maker from Erie, Pa., meets the hip gal from Los Angeles with a master's degree in psychology. She wore black suede boots and shiny red leather heels. I wore white socks and docksiders.

While my occupation was somewhat easy to explain—manufacturing—I, along with most of her family, really didn't "get" what Heidi did for a living.

As the months went by in our coast-to-coast relationship, while visiting in L.A., I would occasionally be invited to attend some of her business conferences and networking meetings.

And what I witnessed really blew me away.

I had no idea that entrepreneurs, like me, could benefit from not only attending local business networking meetings but that there was truly an art to the secrets of meeting new connections and actually getting new clients from them. Like anything else, learning how to meet with people and really connect is a skill. Some people are naturally good at it, but most really aren't.

The next step to being a sterling communicator? Learning how to speak in public. Most people would rather die than be asked to say a few words in front of a funeral gathering. Come to think of it, that's actually kind of funny in a twisted sort of way. Just trade places!

But Heidi's true calling has always been in *empowering women* to step out of their comfort zone and to lead a much more fulfilling and impactful life. As her de-facto producer for almost 20 years, I've witnessed the incredible transformation of hundreds of women through her powerful networking events, seminars, and private coaching clients.

I've literally watched her teach shy and introverted women to become powerful and successful speakers, motivators, and entrepreneurs.

I've watched her work with Fortune 500 companies, helping women managers and executives become more confident and assertive as they climb the corporate ladder.

And I've watched her work with women who felt underappreciated and unnoticed, helping them become the exact opposite by leaning into who they truly are, loving it, and showing others in their lives that they are here to play bigger.

The word "authentic" is sometimes overused, but I can assure you that, in Heidi's case, it is not. She's done her own personal growth work and has the degrees and the experience in real life to make a difference in yours.

It's been one of the joys of my life to watch this marvelous, witty, smart, beautiful, and caring woman change lives on a daily basis.

I'm quite confident that she can change yours for the better, also.

Sincerely,

Phil Kerner

(AKA "My Guy" from Erie)

A woman's most beautiful outfit is confidence.

Her prettiest accessory is charisma.

The most fabulous shoes she could wear are the ones that

Let her walk into any room with courage.

~Heidi Parr Kerner

Opening Act – Creating the Script for Your Success

I believe your life's journey led you to this book. Whatever your age, background, or stage in life, I'm certain you are here, right now, because you're supposed to be. Our paths have crossed for a reason. You have an adventurous spirit and are ready—at last—to make your dreams a reality.

Maybe you have been in your career for years and long to be a leader in your company or niche. Maybe you are a stay-at-home mom who longs to bring up her great ideas at PTA meetings or around your family. Maybe you are dealing with some stressful issues at work or home and just long to speak your mind, finally be heard!

You might be thinking that all those women are incredibly different from each other, but they aren't really. They are all dealing with a really common issue: they lack some skills that can help them take charge of their careers, their personal lives, or their love lives and start living the way they want, authentically as themselves, instead of smashing their desires deep down inside of them.

Whatever your reality is, this book is about helping you reconnect with yourself, discovering what an amazing and dynamic woman you are and becoming the star of your own life so you can live that life to the fullest, without holding back.

Rediscovering your authentic self takes strength, courage, and a whole lot of vulnerability, but the results will exceed your wildest expectations. Want to feel more joyful? Want to wake up every day with gratitude? Want to walk with pride and intention? You can! Gaining self-esteem and having hope for the future is possible; sometimes all you need is a guiding light for your journey ... and a little company along the way.

Over the past 30 years, I have worked with thousands of women, with tons of different dreams and goals, enabling them to remove their social masks and encouraging them to lead a more authentic life. Having a master's degree in psychology and experience as a certified career coach, workshop leader, and former therapist—as well as my own journey of personal development, including self-development classes, workshops, books, seminars, and many coaches and mentors—has taught me what a gentle push can do to help seekers find the courage to make time for themselves and discern what they truly want.

I take my work as a mentor and coach seriously, so I recognize that growing means different things to different people. Each client is special, unique, and my role is to enable them to play bigger.

Many of my clients are interested in becoming more confident communicators and are hungry to learn professional development tools such as assertive communication, public speaking, networking, and leadership skills to empower them, strengthen their credibility, and enhance their social skills. For some, it's to help them create better relationships at home, whether it's time-management skills or how to create a better life balance. For some, it's dating and finding love. For others, they are seeking a tribe of like-minded women who will support them personally and professionally, but they need help getting to a place where they feel comfortable showing up for networking or even a play date.

The journey toward a happier life comes with a price, though. Reaching beyond one's comfort zone, trying out new behaviors, and thinking differently is easier said than done. I always remind my clients, "You must believe and trust the process," a sentiment I lived out fully while writing this book and working with an editor for the first time. The biggest problem I see while working with women, no matter their present situation, is that they lose their sense of self and motivation to make things better in their lives.

Where are they losing themselves? Work, family, friends, volunteering, even in binge-watching TV shows. Somewhere along the way, the dreams of our youth end up pushed aside as we strive to serve others at the cost of ourselves.

Let me explain—often, there's a whisper in their soul that something is not right, and yet, they take no action. I call this the "busy disease." They're too busy to find a new career. They're too busy to navigate a new wardrobe and hairstyle. They're too busy to take that trip, start that class, begin that book. They are even too busy to make a commitment to find *the one*. Simply put, they're too busy to invest in themselves. It's a sickness that is the result of feeling like you're not good enough or that you don't deserve the time to build the life you want—the one you imagined as a child—but it's not until you're ready to grow that you can seek a more fulfilling life. I learned that the hard way.

You may be wondering how I wrote the script for my own success. How did I go from a self-proclaimed uncool, introverted 13-year-old—never gathering the courage to talk to the boy who stood by me at the bus stop for three years and always cowering to bullies—to a motivational speaker who inspires women to play bigger? How did I have the confidence to become a business consultant and an executive coach working with entrepreneurs and top executives in Fortune 100 and 500 companies? How did I step into a leadership role in my community and become the recipient of Women Making History 2019, a prestigious award created by the Mercy Center in Erie, Pa., honoring women who make a difference in their community. And lastly, how on earth does one find the courage to never give up on love and marry for the first time at age 43?

I went from a woman who was so shy that she would literally hide in restrooms prior to business meetings—fearful of intermingling—to a confident, inspiring coach. When once I ran out of theater auditions (even though in my heart I longed to be an actress), I later learned to face my stage fright, moved to Los Angeles, Calif., and became a stand-in for a popular television show. I've learned to find true love at any age, even when society deemed it impossible, and to deal with unimaginable loss, blended families, and broken dreams. I learned to direct my own life and step into the spotlight. I wrote my own script because I knew, deep down, that I was the only one who could. But I had to make some changes and build the foundation to get where I was meant to go!

In this book, I will share with you my somewhat complicated journey to happiness and success. I'll introduce you to my "sisters"— Confidence, Charisma, and Courage—

and teach you how they can be there for you too, guiding you through every act in your life, both professionally and personally. They will equip you for your journey and inspire you to meet the love of your life (or ignite the love you already have). They will teach you to walk into any room and enjoy the reception you receive. They will instill in you the ability to stop taking things personally, speak up for yourself, say *no*, reach outside of your comfort zone, and play bigger.

We'll tackle issues that keep us from examining ourselves and living lives of authenticity: what gets in the way, why we fall into those roles, and what we can do to play different ones. I'll share stories of women I've had the opportunity to work with and how they have stepped into their spotlight and are now playing bigger! I will show you how to write your own script for success and take your life back.

Every journey has both joy and pain, so when sharing my own personal heartaches, losses, and disappointments, I'm also sharing my successes and personal triumphs. My hope is that, as you read these stories, you will recognize parts of yourself that are ready to be seen. Remember, you are not alone, and it's never too late to become who you were meant to be.

Finally, I'll share my Inspirational Toolboxes filled with tools, tips, and techniques to encourage and empower you to live your dreams. I'll be by your side coaching you and believing in you, your capabilities, and your gifts. I will help you write your own script for success.

I know firsthand what it's like to feel shy and uncomfortable in your own skin, hiding in the background, not going after the life goals you set long ago, and feeling like your dreams and aspirations aren't possible, or worse, don't matter. We each have a story to tell, but it takes courage and vulnerability to share one's heart with others. If you're willing, my experience and the support of other women can help you find the new and more fulfilling life that is waiting for you. A new day is dawning ... a new day for all your dreams to come true!

Prologue: Meet Sisters Confidence, Charisma, and Courage

When I conduct my seminars, I always ask my audience how many of them want more confidence and charisma. Without fail, 99% of the audience raises their hands.

Growing up, my family and I moved a total of six times before I graduated high school. In each new home, the first thing I did was scout out the basement for my stage. For me, it was all about the curtain. Without it, I couldn't be a star. After deciding where my stage would go, it was always the same dance: my mother would willingly bring down drapes or shower curtains and my father would reluctantly hang them. Only then did I feel safe and secure in my new home.

There was safety in creating my own stage, my familiar props, and costumes at hand, but I longed to play on a bigger stage—a real stage. The problem was that I didn't have the confidence. My shyness was excruciating. I wanted to be seen, yet I was terrified of that exact scenario. It didn't make sense to me: How can one create a literal stage in their home, yet not have the confidence to perform? My will to perform was strong, but I didn't know how to step into the spotlight!

I envied my classmates who were outwardly confident and seemingly comfortable with who they were. Conversely, I longed to be someone else—someone with that *magic* that attracts people to you. I didn't know the word at the time, but what my classmates possessed—and I did not—was *charisma.*

At 15 years old, after my father announced that we were moving from Syracuse, New York, to Erie, Pa., I made a decision that would change my life forever. I heard a whisper in my soul that this was my time to step up and play bigger. It was my time to set my own real-life stage. I was finally ready to let go of that quiet, nerdy girl and step into the spotlight! But I knew I couldn't do it alone. This is when I found the confidence, charisma, and courage within myself to make changes. I call them *the sisters* because whatever occurs in my life, they are always there to guide me.

The eldest sister, Confidence, is the head. She is disciplined, strict. Confidence is good at keeping you on task and true to your character. She helps you *act the part:* reminding you to practice walking with your head held high, talking to yourself in the mirror so you can speak clearly and authentically, and wearing different costumes that embody your character.

Charisma, the middle sister, is the heart(beat). She reminds us, *Smile! It's show time!* Charisma walks into a room, and people flock to her. Why? What magic does she possess? With Sister Confidence by her side, Charisma enjoys attention. She looks people in the eye, making everyone she meets feel special. She is enthusiastic. She has open body language. People are drawn to her and want what she has, like fans lining the red carpet hoping to brush up against some celebrity star power. Charisma is a special trait, and I am here to tell you, you can have it too! The good news is that you don't have to be born with it; you can develop it.

And Courage? She's the soul of this operation and moves us into action. Even as the youngest sister, she's the bravest of them all. Courage pushes Confidence and Charisma out of their comfort zones. Courage says, *Walk into that new school like you are walking the red carpet*. Without Courage, Confidence's and Charisma's efforts are in vain. It is important to remember that these three sisters work together.

For example, I can be confident in making a marketing video because of my training and expertise, but Charisma makes sure I'm smiling, making great eye contact, and using open body language, drawing others to me. It takes Courage to present myself, and my work, to the world. It takes Courage to be vulnerable. Confidence is an outside job, Charisma is an inside job, and Courage is what pushes us out of our comfort zones and into action. They are family. Each contributes a special gift, and together they provide a roadmap to a more authentic and dynamic life. Let me explain further.

Confidence owns who she is and is secure in her actions. She knows how to garner respect from others. Confidence says *yes* to opportunities, and if things don't work out at first, she helps us try again. She's self-aware, smart, logical, and direct! She trusts herself and can be blunt. She does not easily surrender her authority and sometimes has difficulty connecting to others, but she is successful in her own right. Confidence is a leader and always in control.

Charisma wants to connect. She's hungry for attention, and because of her enthusiasm, she easily attracts people to her. She likes to have fun. She's learned to ingratiate herself to others quickly and easily. She nudges her older sister to loosen up, *We got this,* she says. *Let's stay playful; let's be vulnerable. Let's smile and see where that takes us. Let's be curious about others.* Owning your charisma is a valuable and vulnerable attribute. What we're really saying to others when we're charismatic is, *I see you and I'm allowing you to see me.* Charisma is fully engaging in life. It's about coming from the heart and a place of presence.

Courage is the risk-taking daredevil. She is strong and unafraid to fight for what she wants. She's a little scrappy at times, but with Charisma by her side, she becomes softer. Courage pushes us to use our confidence and charisma in ways we never imagined. We need Courage to ask for what we want! Maybe it's a raise. Or standing up and being assertive with a coworker. Courage helps us to set boundaries and to say "no" with grace. Courage says, "That's enough." I no longer care what people think. Courage says this job, relationship, or where I live doesn't work for me anymore. It's time to move on and take inspired action! We need Courage to communicate clearly with others instead of brushing matters under the rug. We need courage when we are experiencing grief, loss or sickness. Courage, more than anything, dictates our life's journey. She is our soul. Courage is the energy bringing together all our pieces for our best life.

There are lots of successful, uncharismatic people, you may be thinking. And to that I say, *Of course there are!* You can certainly be confident and not have charisma. You can possess all the confidence and charisma in the world and never do anything with it because you lack courage. But the key to *fully* realizing your dreams and playing bigger is to get all three sisters working together for your success. Show a confident smile, embody a charismatic presence, and use your courage to do whatever it is that makes you happy and fulfilled. That's the message of this book: learn to love yourself first, and then you'll find that others will respond to you in new and exciting ways.

It's human nature to want others to like you. What doesn't come so easily, however, is starting conversations and communicating (verbally and non-verbally) in a way that attracts people to you. For many, our need for others to like us is often met with anxiety, and we can fall into people pleasing. As children, we ran up to a playmate at the sandbox and dug right in. As adults, there's a bit more nuance, and a lot more self-doubt. Sometimes our lack of communication skills, low self-esteem, and inherent shyness prevent us from experiencing the fullness of life, love, and friendships. In fact, we're so good at remaining fearful about our emotional responses and worried about what others think of us that we forget to enjoy life altogether! It's safer to melt into a corner while attending a social or professional event than to extend a hand and start a conversation. *Maybe no one will notice me,* we think. I'm here to tell you that it doesn't need to be this way. Many people believe you are born with characteristics like confidence, charisma, and courage. I say you can cultivate them. Developing these three traits will become your secret weapon in building more happiness in all areas of your life. How do I know? *Because I did it.*

Adopting sisters Confidence, Charisma, and Courage into your family will change your life. These critical success characteristics do not come naturally to everyone. Be patient. Practice calling on them. It takes work, time, and intention to hone these skills; however, once you learn the practical steps to embrace and celebrate your new family, you will find it so much easier to achieve your goals and live your happiest and most fulfilling life. It's OK to be seen. It's OK to take up space. It's OK to speak up and have a voice. The sisters give you permission to live authentically.

I can't wait to share how the skills and tools I learned in theater (and as a therapist) have helped me develop my sense of self and have helped my clients do the same. Whether it's encouraging them to dress differently (wear a new costume), practice a new skill ("the illusion of the first time," which means to present your best self every time), use a prop (waving a magic wand), dance or play (opening up and experimenting), these tools are proven to work. I've helped women step into their spotlight and own their stage, living lives beyond their wildest dreams. My hope is that reading their stories will inspire you to do the same in your own life.

Now, let's get on with the show!

Jane

Jane lives her life on her own terms and on her own stage. Let me share her story with you.

I was attending the grand opening of a local restaurant in our community when I heard, "Hi Heidi. It's Jane!" The voice seemingly came out of nowhere. *Darn,* I thought. Whenever I saw this woman in the community, she always introduced herself to me. The problem? I could never remember who she was, and truth be told, she didn't exactly stand out in a crowd: medium height, brunette with a plain hairstyle, casual clothing, no makeup, a flat facial expression. Her presence seemed to say, *Please don't notice me.*

Worried my face possessed the, *You look familiar, but I can't place you* expression, I quickly said *hello* back and suggested we have a coffee date to get to know one another. I was pleasantly surprised when she mentioned she was interested in participating in the upcoming women's empowerment group I was hosting—a six-month program of personal and professional development.

Jane was an avoidant. She hid around others and was uncomfortable in her own skin. However, at the time, she was also a seasoned and accomplished journalist and editor. She was a gifted writer and took refuge in the written word. Even though she loved writing, I sensed a pull that she wanted something different. I can recall her first empowerment group meeting. The women were chatty and excited to meet each other, connect, and ask questions, but Jane sat by herself, looking at papers, checking her phone. She was literally isolating herself by sitting apart from other members. Frankly, she appeared somewhat aloof and disinterested. She seemed like she did not want to be present, yet she came. There must be some need or want in her life, I thought, that brought her to my class.

During an exercise where we revealed our *masks* (a figurative prop we use to hide our true selves), Jane was vulnerable and shared that the mask she wore was symbolic of hiding herself: hiding from others, from what she truly wanted from life, and from what she really wanted to do professionally.

As mentioned, my theater and therapy background have influenced me greatly, leading me to believe in the power of picking a role model, someone you look up to. You admire the characteristics, look, energy, and essence of this person. You want to be more like them. You like how they speak or carry themselves or dress.

When we give ourselves permission to be another "character," such as our role model, sometimes it feels safer to explore areas of ourselves we never would when we are "being ourselves."

Why do you think so many of us enjoy Halloween? Trying on a different look, wig, costume, and yes mask, changes our persona! It can be FUN to experiment with different parts of ourselves that might be dormant. Why not use this tool as part of your exploration and your inner journey?

For example, in the past when I have created videos for my social media, I often would get stuck. I tried sometimes to be too polished. I strived to let my authentic self come out, but my "perfectionist mask" came out instead. I knew it. I could feel it. I had a disconnect between who I was being and who I wanted to be.

So I brought in Marie Osmond! She's a singer, actress, and author who I grew up watching and admiring. Marie had a talk show around the time that I was working on my video persona, and she was so open with her vulnerability that I wanted to be her! She easily cried, was always quick to laugh at herself, and truly cared about her audience.

When I stumbled in my videos, I started (as I like to say) "channeling Marie Osmond." How would Marie sit? What would she say? How would she dress? Act? I've threatened to one day release my "blooper reels," where you can hear me say, "I am Marie Osmond," in between takes to prove the point that this works!

I used to need ten takes to create a one-minute video. Now with Marie on my side—someone who already embodies my three sisters, Confidence, Charisma, and Courage—I'm a one-take wonder! Thanks Marie!

During my group meetings, the attendees can relate to theses role model exercises as confidence boosters! They can "take off" their mask, yet feel safe by role playing as their mother, their aunt, an actress, or whoever they see as their ideal self.

Such was the case for Jane. I asked her to attend our next meeting dressed as her role model. Jane walked into our next meeting in a sleek black dress hugging her model-slim body. She looked chic with her hair tucked into a French twist, a strand of pearls at her throat, sophisticated heels, and bright red lipstick. As it turns out, Jane's inner fashion icon was Audrey Hepburn, a vast contrast to her everyday dress of casual T-shirts and jeans. None of us realized what an innate beauty she was. "Oh Jane," I exclaimed, "There you are!" We were dazzled.

So, what happened to Jane? Sometime after her graduation from my class, I heard my name in the grocery store. I walked right by the person without recognizing her, thinking I was imagining someone calling my name. Or was it because I wasn't wearing my glasses? I turned. It was Jane, now a stunning blonde with a fashionable haircut. She was dressed stylishly and making eye contact. She seemed different, and then I realized Jane finally took off her mask. We briefly caught up, and she told me that she found the courage to change careers. She was now a nurse. Finally, at the age of 50, she found the confidence and courage to be her most authentic self. Amazing wonders will happen for you too if you listen to your inner self and your newfound sisters.

The sisters helped Jane change her life. Let's take a closer look at how it all works. Confidence comes from structures we learn on the outside (like dressing as your favorite classy icon) and knowledge we gain over the years. Charisma taps the heart; it gives you permission to be authentic and lead with the heart. Courage moves you from what you learned or know to inspired action. All three walk hand in hand, supporting one another. Yes, it will take time and effort, but believe me, it's worth it. If you are reading this book right now, you clearly want more: more joy, more happiness, more success. You want to push yourself out of your comfort zone and live life to its greatest potential. Adopting the sisters Confidence, Charisma, and Courage into your life can help you realize this potential.

Act I

Setting the Stage: Where it All Began

Scene 1 – Meet My Parents

My parents were brought up with completely different backgrounds. I believe their upbringing directly influenced the two parts of me I see played out in every area of my life. It's fair to say that my mother grew up in a family of means. My dad's background was vastly different. He had a simple upbringing, nothing fancy. His family was very frugal yet resourceful.

My mother, Miss Manners—think Mary Poppins, *practically perfect in every way*—taught me the art of social graces, organizational skills, adherence to protocol. Put your napkin on your lap once you sit down at the table, always write a thank you note, dress from head to toe and make your bed every day. She matched up with my dad, Mr. Sociability, with an *everybody is my friend* mindset exuding confidence, charisma, and humor, which was a little naughty at times. I inherited my father's gift of engaging with others. Every person is special. Always have a strong handshake. Look people in the eye. Smile. He was networking at its finest.

He was the life of the party, always had a funny joke to share, and was known for calling his friends to remind them when it was his birthday!

How did this unlikely pair meet and fall in love?

Theirs is a classic love story. This story—and others in this chapter—set the stage for my life.

Springtime in Paris

After studying for five years to become a Catholic priest, my father, originally from Syracuse, New York, left the seminary and joined the armed forces. He was stationed in Paris, France, where he was assigned as an army counterintelligence agent. There, in early spring of 1958, he met my mother: a young woman with an adventurous spirit and a love of travel.

A recent Manhattanville College graduate, my mother was living in Paris and working as an assistant to various American executives and writers, along with writing occasional articles for her hometown Boston newspaper. Possessing a press card provided unlimited opportunities for her. In one such adventure, she accompanied a dear family friend, a *Boston Globe* journalist, to London. She had been assigned by her newspaper to cover the coronation of young Queen Elizabeth II after the death of her father, King George VI. After visiting several other countries, my mother was forever captivated by travel. A wonderful new world always awaited.

My mother's first employer was the acclaimed writer Irwin Shaw, whose movie *The Young Lions* (starring Marlon Brando, Montgomery Cliff, and Dean Martin) was showing in Paris and receiving rave reviews. She lived on the Left Bank in the charming district of Saint-Germain-des-Prés sharing an apartment with her two college roommates: one worked for a motion picture studio and taught English at the American School of Paris, and the other worked for the Defense Department at the American Embassy. My mom and my dad lived in the same neighborhood, enjoyed the same circle of friends, and shared the same interests.

April in Paris. The City of Lights and Romance. Two hearts meet. Young and growing in love, a whirlwind romance ensued. Within months, my dad proposed before the statue of the Blessed Mother at the Cathedral of Saint-Germain-des-Prés, their church.

Within a year's time the young couple returned to the United States, married in Boston surrounded by family and friends, and moved to Staten Island, New York. My dad would take the first ferry boat each morning to his job on Wall Street. At the end of the day, after his law classes at St. John's Law School in the evening, he returned to Staten Island on the last ferry boat of the night. It was 1959. They later described their year of courtship, which ended in marriage, as magical.

My mother never learned to cook, do laundry, iron shirts, prepare late dinners, or navigate the daunting tasks of daily homemaking, yet managed to create a cozy home in their tiny apartment tucked into an old gray Victorian house across from the Staten Island Zoo—all in eager anticipation of my springtime arrival.

My mother was raised in a privileged home environment in Milton, Mass., a suburb outside of Boston. Faith, family, patriotism, hard work, respect, discipline, manners, and proper etiquette were values adhered to at all costs. Her father was a prosperous businessman, as reflected in the family's lifestyle, which included maids, a cook, chauffeur, and gardeners. My mother and her three brothers attended private schools. Daytime schedules were filled with innumerable activities: sports, music, and challenging wildlife camping expeditions for the boys; dance, horses, music, and theater for my mother.

My mother and her dad (my grandfather, Allan Richard White) shared a passion for horses. Both equestrians, horseback riding was their cherished time together. My mom especially enjoyed Sunday afternoon hunts. Riders and their horses would gather in an open field and under the leadership of the Master of the Hunt—a dashing figure in his blazing red fitted coat, white jodhpurs, high black boots, and a black velvet top-hat. The blare of his trumpet would commence the hunt, and a gaggle of yelping hounds would be released from their pens, followed by a medley of hunters and horses in pursuit. Over the stone walls, gurgling streams, wooden fences of varying heights, hills high and low ... wherever the dogs caught the scent, the hunters would follow. Such drama! I would visualize it all as my family shared stories and photos through the years. It was like a Hollywood movie.

In contrast to my mother's experience of growing up with privilege, my dad's childhood was filled with warmth and focused on family. He was an only child, born and raised in Syracuse, New York. His parents were devoted and hardworking. Depression years. Financial woes. Lots of moving. He was always adjusting to new schools, neighborhoods, and churches. His mother was an avid gardener and an exceptional cook. Her recipes were always in demand, and children were constantly coming and going in their small but welcoming homes.

As the result of his modest upbringing, my dad often made items he needed or wanted, including his first pair of skis. For several years, his family lived in a mobile home located by a prestigious golf course where my dad caddied.

"I'm going to be a member there one day," he'd tell people. His fantasy became a reality.

Despite the different lifestyles my parents experienced in their early years, they always remained a team, working together to raise their young family with love and support. Even through many moves without the help of friends or family and no financial assistance, they remained strong. Sometimes, as the years passed, I wondered if the love and devotion my parents shared would be possible for me. Would I ever know the enduring intensity of such a relationship? Would I ever experience my own story of romance? In my yearning for deep love, and questioning if ever it would be mine, did I still dare to dream?

My dad, a banker and lawyer, was a proud and active member of our community. He was president of the local Rotary Club, and he belonged to countless boards and organizations including The United Way and The Serra Club. When I was 16, I recall attending a Rotary ceremony honoring him for his many achievements. Tall, handsome, charismatic, comfortable with himself, and using humor when appropriate, he was the epitome of the ideal speaker. He had my respect and admiration. I wondered if I would share in such gifts one day.

Fast forward some years later, my dad developed Parkinson's disease. Learning there was no support in Erie for this challenging disorder—not even a pamphlet—I sent him informational material from Los Angeles where I lived. I had become involved with a wonderful support group for patients and families. I wondered quietly if he would be interested in starting a support group in Erie.

I knew there was nothing close by to support my parents with this new diagnosis of Parkinson's disease, so with a little more nudging, my parents created the first support group in Erie. I imagine they needed support from their own sisters Confidence, Charisma, and Courage! I was so proud of them and happy I could make a difference even though it was from afar. A small group of several couples gathered at my parents' home, each feeling so alone, uninformed, and frightened. On that crisp fall morning in 1992, the seeds for the foundation of The Parkinson Partners of NWPA, Inc. were planted. Thirty years later, and enormously expanded, it continues to bring support, education, hope, and help in Erie and NW Pennsylvania to innumerable families. The legacy of James H. Parr lives on.

Theirs was a beautiful love story that ended too abruptly. However, my parents provided a strong foundation that allowed me to become the person I am today. I continue to share the lessons I learned from them with my own family, friends, and clients.

Growing up in our home, there was always room and regard for others. There was also discipline, spiritual values to be adhered to, and manners to be observed. *Children should be seen and not heard* was an unspoken generational adage. During these transformational years, I believe, I took this phrase to heart and retreated into a world of shyness, quiet, and low self-esteem that I would battle for years.

My Childhood Stage

Although shy, my inner performer needed an outlet, so my home became my stage. I was the creative director leading my five younger siblings in neighborhood theatrical productions, musicals, and carnivals. My brothers and sisters didn't know it yet, but they were my performers. My props consisted of outdated clothing my mom gave us that she no longer wore—hats (lots of hats), evening gowns, purses, and black shiny pumps that felt so elegant. I loved my costumes; they gave me permission to play and helped ignite my imagination.

It was always the same cast of characters: my five younger brothers and sisters and our neighborhood friend Britney. Britney lived across the street and was right in the middle, age-wise, of all of us. Our plays were mostly based on what was happening in our lives. I remember my mother was less than thrilled when she caught us *playing church* one time, each actor taking communion.

My favorite play of all time (and still is) was around Christmas when I put my brother Michael into the role of Santa Claus. Britney was instructed by me to act as the reindeer. Since we didn't have a bridle and harness available, we found some nylon rope by my Dad's workbench in the basement that we secured around her neck as she pulled the sleigh, while our skinny Santa belly-laughed and threw gifts out into the audience. Britney's mother came running over to the house later that day and scolded me as Britney came home with rope burns around her neck. Whoops. Lesson learned.

Our lives were back and forth between Britney's house and ours. Britney's mom, Linda, was also our piano teacher. I enjoyed playing the piano until it was time to perform in front of an audience. When it came time for the recital, I announced clearly that day to my mother, "I'm not going." Despite her bribing and encouragement, I insisted I wouldn't go. At the last possible minute, she dragged me across the street in my pretty pink chiffon dress, looking angry.

According to my mother, I was "outstanding." Even so, stage fright would continue to haunt me through the years. Even to this day, whether I'm conducting a speaking engagement, creating a video, or getting up in front of others, the jitters are still with me. There are times I would rather crawl up in a ball and go to bed because I just don't want to do it. But my sister Courage pushes me out of my comfort zone and reminds me, I must play BIGGER to make an impact. I do it. And once I get over that initial fear, I step into my power and remind myself that this is fun. It's *show time*, Heidi!

You might be wondering, where did all this theater and performing come from? What about all the costumes? I know this isn't necessarily the norm in every family. However, in our family playing dress up and taking photos was something we were basically raised with. Every year my parents created a Christmas card, and the Parr kids were the performers who played the characters. It was always a nativity scene. I was dressed up as Mary, my brother played Joseph, and the newest Parr baby was always Jesus (in my arms). My other siblings? Some played the angels, and my brother played the wine connoisseur, with a real bottle of wine! My Dad, an amateur photographer, loved creating these scenes. And with my mother's flair for the creative, they were *scenes*! One year, they rented a real donkey for the photoshoot, and it took off running while I was riding it. Mary was not happy.

But even with performing for my parents and the piano recitals in my early years, my reluctance to socialize continued. I was so shy and reticent as a child, my mother told me that if I would just say *hello* to the boy I waited with at the bus stop each morning, she would reward me with a dollar. "Practice, Heidi dear, just practice," she would say.

Living in the country, it was sometimes a long wait for the bus. "H-E-L-L-O, BEN," she would repeat and repeat again, enunciating each sound. I tried, but I was never successful. Ever. To this day I wonder what would have happened if I broke through my fear and actually said his name aloud.

I felt tall and awkward growing up. I couldn't understand when adults would say, "How pretty you are!" I didn't have many friends. My fellow classmates teased me and said I was a "geek." I was. I was shy. I didn't know how to talk. I was scared. During gym class, I was the last selected to join a team. I was bullied. I felt embarrassed, ashamed. I felt I was never good enough. My mother enrolled me in the Barbizon School of Modeling to give me more confidence and so I could learn to embrace my height. Still, I was unable to conquer my fear of talking ... to anyone.

Sisters Confidence and Courage were nowhere to be found.

My anxiety was so intense, I developed anxiety ticks. I would throw my head back, making weird faces, my shoulders making jolting movements. "Stop doing that," my father would say with concern mingled with annoyance, but I had no control. My mother even admitted to sitting outside my classroom to observe if this was just something that happened at home or if it also happened while I was away. To her dismay, I was doing it in the classroom too. At that time, classes were very large, and the medical field made no connections between stress and mental health. We didn't talk about my behavior, and the ticks finally subsided later in life.

As I entered my teen years, I developed a secretive eating disorder: compulsive eating then starving myself and excessively exercising. My food and body image issues left me even more introverted. If you tend to be an introvert, you know we like watching and observing others. I quietly studied how the popular kids presented and acted. I didn't know what confidence felt like, but I saw what it looked like!

Maria Jones was blonde, statuesque, and beautiful. She was an avid swimmer (with a swimmer's body) and when she smiled, she lit up a room. All the girls wanted to be her friend, and all the boys wanted to go steady with her. A posse followed her wherever she went. She talked, walked, and chatted so freely and confidently with her peers. She dressed in style. She had confidence, no doubt, and that added sparkle that made her seem magical. Maria had *charisma.* She made everybody feel special. She attracted people with her smile, the way she included people, and her leadership. I wanted a posse. I wanted stylish clothes. I wanted to sparkle. Little did I know, the opportunity to change my look, and attitude, was right around the corner (or should I say, *state*).

When I was 15, my father announced that the family was moving to a new city: Erie, Pa., because of a bank merger. When he first told me, I went ballistic—there was a lot of screaming, door slamming, and crying (I was a typical teenager). Yet, in time, something within me quietly whispered, *Now is your chance, Heidi. Nobody will know you at your new school. This could be a fresh start. You can become a different you. You can sparkle. You can dazzle.* I called on my sister Courage. This was it. It was my time to SHINE. I needed her help to take action and play out my new part!

A New City, A New Me

I made a conscious decision: at my new school, I would become popular. I already studied the popular kids in my area, how they acted and how they dressed. Now all I needed to do was apply my "act *as if*" attitude at my new school. On my first day at my new school in Erie I walked into classes with new clothes, a new hairstyle, a new walk, a new confident inner voice, and awareness of how others perceived me. I practiced all summer, and I was hoping my hard work would pay off.

The funny part was that a large component of how I boosted my confidence was through mirror work (I just didn't know it was called "mirror work" yet). I spoke positively to myself in the mirror pretending to be confident. I pretended I was Maria Jones. And it worked. At school, I acted hip and cool and projected confidence and charisma with flair. Something wondrous happened that day: I was a teenager on a tenuous journey to self-discovery. Throughout the next couple of years, I found my voice. There was so much locked inside that I needed to share. It was my time to speak out and be heard. And I liked it. Everybody wanted to be my friend. The first day of school as the new girl, I felt liked and accepted and like a star. Phew! It was working. I thought to myself, *I've got something going on here with this confidence and charisma stuff!*

I loved my high school years. I attended dances and social events. I had boyfriends. Lots of them. (To this day, I remain close to many of my first friends from Erie.) During this time, I vowed to myself that no matter how scared I got in the future—or how embarrassed I might feel—I would always remember my ability to create confidence in myself. I could play a role; I could choose how I wanted to present myself to the world. There was a different way of living life, and I didn't need shyness and insecurity to define it. I felt a sense of power when I created my own confidence, and I loved the results. That fall, I went off to Ithaca College. It was 1978, and though that quiet, shy girl resided in me, I was hoping Confidence, Charisma, and Courage would be by my side. I was about to experience an unanticipated happening.

Scene 2 – Discovering My Purpose

I was genuinely excited to venture into my college years. Finally, I felt ready to live on my own! Little did I imagine that the shy, introverted little girl of yesteryear would pop up again in my life and take over center stage. *But I have confidence now, right?*

My parents drove me to Ithaca College on a beautiful late summer day. Ithaca is nestled among rolling hills in the Finger Lakes region of upstate New York. It's a quiet college town with a bit of an art-scene. I was eager to know all the fabulous people acting on my new stage. Once there, we immediately began unloading our van overflowing with my possessions, making our way up the three flights of stairs to my assigned dorm room.

As I walked toward my room, carrying an enormous dress bag, I paused, peeking inside. There she was, my roommate, but instead of waving *hello*, I quickly turned and walked away. My walk turned into a run as I made my way down the long, narrow corridor, stopping my parents in their tracks as they slowly approached. "I'm. Not. Staying!" I announced defiantly, clearly enunciating each word. My dad, carrying my new desk, sweating, not in any mood to deal with my shenanigans, replied under his breath, "Like hell you're not." My mother, more compassionate, but displaying total disbelief, practically dropped her huge box of linens. Regaining her balance, pushing her dark hair off her face, she tried to register the words I was saying. “Heidi, Heidi dear. What happened?”

My anxiety was back.

Sally

I peeked into my room again. There, sitting on the bed, was a girl who hardly portrayed my fantasy of a dream roommate. I’ll be honest with you, I was extremely judgmental of this young woman at the time, but for the sake of transparency, I’m going to share with you how I really felt. The truth was she looked boring and drab to me. I could tell she would not want to join me at parties, chat about boys, and get into a little good trouble. I didn’t want to act fake and befriend her, and I knew there was a slim chance of having anything in common. I returned to my mother sulking even more, but despite my ranting, my parents stuck to their guns, maintaining, “Heidi, you are here to stay. Give it a chance. It will work out. If not, then ...” That was it; I picked my poison, and it was time to drink it. In a flurry of tearful hugs, kisses, and *I love yous*, my parents left as fast as they came. I never felt so alone, so abandoned.

As I expected, Sally and I seemingly shared nothing in common: music, clothes, boys, educational pursuits. You name it. Nothing. Things didn’t change as the semester went on. We did arrange and maintain our room together. We were cordial. But we hardly spoke. My mother and friends from Erie who went off to various colleges became accustomed to me calling them at all hours of the day and night. *Ring. Ring. Ring.* Silence. Then, “Is it you, Heidi?” More silence on my end followed by sobbing, followed by, “I hate it here. I want to come home.” More sobbing. I asked my friends, "Do you hate college as much as I do?" They couldn't lie. They were quickly making new friends and having a wonderful time. Once again alone. Once again, a geek. No confidence in sight. I felt like a yo-yo of emotions: I was so happy and confident just a few short weeks prior, and now, so unhappy and ashamed of who I was. The problem was that I didn't know how to express these feelings; I just knew I didn't want to feel this way anymore.

Everybody at Ithaca looked so different from me. Many of the students were from New York City. The girls wore tight Jordache jeans, high heels, and lots of makeup. They quickly formed cliques. The guys wore cologne, used hairspray, and dressed fastidiously. I was used to blue-collar guys who thought I was wonderful with my natural long hair and casual style of dress. I didn't realize what a country bumpkin I truly was. Erie wasn't the smallest of towns, but it certainly wasn't pulling in New Yorkers over the weekend. The closest large cities to Erie are Cleveland, Buffalo, and Pittsburgh. The general atmosphere among men in the Rust Belt was less Sinatra and more Springsteen. I honestly felt like I was in a foreign country—and I knew I wasn't fitting in—until I met Ann.

Ann

One day, as I was waiting in line at the school cafeteria for my tuna melt, I noticed a short, jolly-looking girl standing next to me. With her big, brown eyes staring up at me she said, "Hi! I love the tuna melts here, too. I'm Ann. What's your name?" I was instantly relieved. The tight knot in my throat loosened. My hands unclenched. I felt, for the first time since arriving at school, at ease. Ann didn't look like those other girls: she was in a simple T-shirt, shorts, and flip flops. I noticed she wasn't wearing a bra. Earth mama? Feminist? I was curious.

We became fast friends. She was like a breath of fresh air. She was Jewish. I was Catholic. Coming from Erie, I was unfamiliar with Jewish traditions. There's a small Jewish population in Erie, but I didn’t have any Jewish friends growing up, and I was curious to know everything about her: her heritage, her culture, her spiritual beliefs, her interests. She introduced me to new foods (I’d never tasted a bagel before), to the concept of speaking your truth and honoring your authentic self, and to her wonderful, warm, welcoming New England family. The thing that struck me most about Ann was how she spoke up for herself. If she didn't like something she ordered at a restaurant, she sent it back. I never knew anyone like that, especially another young woman. I was brought up to be quiet, demure, and yes, passive. Just when I felt confidence had forsaken me, Ann arrived in my life. A real live role model reflecting confidence and charisma.

Life at Ithaca took on a new twist. I had a friend! We attended concerts, theatrical productions, sporting events, and lectures together. We even took classes together. In time, a circle of fascinating and diverse new friends evolved. Ithaca College became comfortable and interesting. I was even having fun! After that first tenuous year, Ann and I roomed together for the remainder of our college years. We lived and worked summers together on Cape Cod and smoked pot for the first time together (don’t tell our parents). Ann worked at a popular hamburger joint. I worked as a chambermaid (yuck) and did some waitressing.

By my second year of college, Ann and I had truly found our tribe, and in honor of my intense Jewish training,

Ann, and some other girls, proclaimed with great sincerity that I was a CAP (Catholic American Princess). I felt included and accepted! Our social circle continued to expand. And what about Sally, my first roommate? In fact, she was quite sweet and very smart. It worked out for everyone in the end. College 101: never judge a book by its cover.

It wasn't until my third year in college that I found my passion. In doing so, some of my confidence returned. The career assessment tests I took each indicated the same results: working with people. A spiritual component was inferred. I thought about maybe becoming a nun. (I giggle at that now.) Probably not, but another area of introspection interested me: sociology. I finally knew my purpose, and the best part was that I could take simple measures to fulfill this purpose.

In my first sociology class, I learned the importance of running groups: how to use them as a tool to process emotions and face challenges. This is when I realized I wanted to work in a social work environment. I loved the drama of role-playing, using my intuition, learning psychology skills, and taking a leadership role. I already experienced many of these skills: being the eldest in a large family, transitioning from a small Pennsylvania community to a large, diverse college atmosphere, travel experiences. My professors encouraged me. I took classes at The Moreno Institute of Psychodrama located in upstate New York, to further enhance my training. Later, I did my internship at Cornell University. There, one of my classes was to enable "overly intellectual" students to improve their social communication skills. To this day, that is part of the work I do with my clients!

Oh, and I want to mention that, as part of my training, I went to clown school—yes there is such a thing—to push myself out of my comfort zone and to be creative. I did somersaults, and the most fun I had was performing mime. We would dress up as clowns and then *hold the space* in the downtown Ithaca promenade as well as the mall. Just like you would think, people would come up and try to make us laugh and distract us. It never worked. We learned the art of being silent and using nonverbal communication.

I learned to find my way during those years and move out of my comfort zone. It was a learning time affecting every facet of my life, the first of many such occasions to follow. I am grateful for the groundwork laid. Ann and I keep in touch, but unfortunately, we seldom see one another. It's consoling to know, though, that at any time, whatever my stage of life, I can pick up the phone to say *hello*, and hear Ann's voice reply, "Oy vey, Heidi, oy vey."

Scene 3 – My Melrose Place

After college in the early 1980s, I moved back to Erie for a couple of years to figure out what I wanted to do next. While there, I worked in the social work field with juvenile delinquent girls at a group home. It impacted my life forever. The girls were young, energetic, and flawed. They teasingly called me *valley girl* even though I had never been to Los Angeles. Little did I know that one day I would call LA my home.

The girls were tough on me. It was a group home environment where I spent the night one to two times a week. When I look back at that time now, it seems innocent; yet drugs, truancy, and stealing were ongoing themes. I learned a lot. Taking girls to court on a regular basis and trying to balance being the counselor, disciplinarian, and a friend they could confide in was a challenge. The excitement of working with the FBI and raiding homes gave me rushes of adrenaline and kept me on my toes. At that time, I felt stuck but knew I wanted to further my education. I started slowly looking into different colleges, yet I felt pretty good being back in Erie. I had reconnected with several of my high school friends, and I was doing some local modeling. I had a job in my field and a boyfriend. I was content.

However, my mother brought us up saying to "leave the nest, travel, move away," which was a very different mindset than most of my Erie friends. Many of my friends in Erie had never traveled, and their family motto was to stay in the safety of their home and community. I secretly longed for that type of family atmosphere. Maybe it was part of my dad's upbringing in me that wanted a simple stay-at-home lifestyle? Yet my mother's influence was strong: get an education and explore the world. And that's what I did! My parents had just traveled back from Los Angeles for a business convention associated with the bank my dad was working for. Upon their return, my mother enthusiastically shared with me, "Heidi, everybody in LA looks like you! They dress differently. They look funky. They are free spirits. You would love it there. LA is where you must go!"

I was a little taken aback; however, with my parents' encouragement, I looked at colleges on the west coast, even though I previously never felt a desire to move to California. I always saw myself as an East Coast gal: busy, energetic, a bit wild. And truly, I didn't really want to move to California. I had my life here in Erie.

Unbeknownst to me at the time, my mother had seen the writing on the wall. I would probably stay in town, get married, and have a great job. However, (to her credit) she wanted *more* for me, and with her Mary Poppins *snap of the fingers* I found myself on a plane to California, accepted at the college of my choice, not quite knowing what hit me. I had never been to California. I moved with reluctance and trepidation. (Um, where are you Courage?) This small-town girl wasn't quite ready for the big city!

Los Angeles

It took little time for reality to set in. I didn't know a soul. I looked in the paper, found an apartment and a roommate, and tried to find a job (and perhaps a small acting role) while starting night classes at Pepperdine University for my graduate degree in psychology. Coming from a small city and small college environment, I felt overwhelmed with the LA lifestyle, yet fascinated. With Confidence by my side I thought, "How hard can this be? I'm qualified for any job I seek."

For my first apartment, my roommate was from New York City. I figured we would have a connection because she was an East Coast girl—and we did. I soon realized I wasn't alone in wanting fame. So many young people move to Los Angeles from their hometown with a suitcase and a dream, but it takes a lot of courage to stay put in the City of Angels. Hollywood's call is loud and her glitz louder. You could feel the buzz of excitement when you stepped onto the streets: a collective subconscious yearning. Sometimes that yearning is a little too much. Most people leave after a year; such was the case with Kerri, my first of many roommates.

My apartment complex looked exactly like a scene out of Melrose Place. The pool dominated the center of the complex with apartments surrounding it. As the weeks went on, other 20-somethings started venturing out on their balconies. We soon had our own troop of transplants with dreams of stardom. We were all ready for the next big break, and it wasn't just the beautiful blondes and handsome hunks looking for fame. No, this is LA, and it seemed like everyone wanted a piece of the pie, regardless of their profession, appearance, or backgrounds. So, even if they were a dentist, accountant, real estate agent, or even a teacher, behind the scenes, most people were taking acting classes, writing a screenplay, and doing all sorts of things while waiting for their discovery. I became one of them, too!

I knew I needed to find a job, and quickly. I applied for a position I saw advertised in a doctor's office as office support. I remember exactly what I wore: turquoise slacks and a matching top. The interview went smoothly until the doctor interviewing me invited me to walk through his large office.

"See how professional my staff looks?" he said, catching me off-guard. "Notice their hair, makeup, the style of their clothing, their shoes. See how attractive they are? That's what we're looking for."

I stared blankly at the slew of beautiful women in front of me. They had style, their hair was perfectly coiffed, and they wore fashionable shoes showing off their slender, tan legs. A pleasant fragrance permeated the space. "If you change your image," my interviewer concluded, "come back."

I was shocked and disappointed, but most of all, humiliated. I felt those familiar feelings of shame come creeping back as reality sank in. I did not fit in here. I wasn't good enough. Frankly, I didn't even know how to dress differently, and I didn't have the money to purchase a new wardrobe. I was alone in the city with no friends or family. Seeing the professional women in their office made me think of the Ithaca girls walking by in their tight jeans and full faces of makeup. I felt so inferior. I felt my confidence retreating. I had allowed myself to feel powerful and beautiful, when in reality I possessed no power or beauty at all in LA. No one was paying attention to me.

I continued my interview circuit, somewhat disheartened, but applied for a position at a law firm. The same thing happened! The attorney who interviewed me pointed out the women in his luxurious office and how they presented themselves. He suggested I grow my hair long.

These interviews proved the adage that in LA, image really is everything. In hindsight, I learned some important lessons about dressing the part, understanding the power of image, and first impressions during this time (we'll talk about dressing a little bit later). In time, I found a wonderful position as a therapist for an in-patient eating disorder clinic. Introduced to their 12-step program, I learned for the first time the *what* and the *why* of this psychological condition. Happily, I could dress the part wearing my peasant skirts and casual blouses—my comfort zone—at least for that period of my life. New friendships developed, and I worked full time as a therapist by day while completing my master's degree in psychology at night. I was on track and ready to have some fun.

In the '80s, Sunset Boulevard was bustling, and everyone—I mean everyone—was inspired by Madonna's wardrobe. The club scene was at its height and so was partying, dancing, late nights, and early morning breakfast at Canter's Restaurant, your typical 24-hour Hollywood diner. My apartment was often packed with a posse of girls getting glam for a night out on the town: spraying our hair as high as it would go, finding the shortest skirts, accessorizing with black lace stockings, gloves, and strands of cheap pearls. We all wanted to be Madonna, and the excitement of what *could be* was exhilarating. (At the time, I thought I'd meet my future husband at a nightclub.) Carlos and Charlie's on Sunset was a popular place to dance. Standing in line with dozens of other young women, we put our confidence on as we coyly flirted with the bouncer in our fishnets and heels.

This is how it worked: the bouncers guarded the red velvet rope, eyeballing the pretty girls, deciding their fate for the evening. If they chose you, you were lucky. A bouncer would dramatically unhook the velvet rope and give you permission to enter the smoky, decadent environment of pounding music, flashing lights, and the scent of heavy cologne on attractive, foreign men. I can still hear the song playing, “Meeting in the Ladies Room,” by Klymaxx and seeing Rick James, Rod Stewart, and George Michael dance the night away. We got in, every time! We were young, reckless, and having the time of our lives.

Most of my weekends were happily spent in clubs dancing with my girlfriends, even though there was always the part of me that was looking for *the one*. Still, it was the mid-’80s, and I wasn’t slowing down anytime soon. I worked day and night, filling my weekends with social activities. I knew it was only a matter of time before the acting bug bit me; Hollywood has a way of sucking you in. I remember the first time I met with a casting agent. I was so nervous that when she asked for my car registration information, I went to my car and guess what? I drove away. I was too shy to audition. But I kept pushing and pursuing. I decided to take acting classes to give me the confidence to try this craft.

I imagined the acting studio for my first class as a huge, dripping-in-gold theater where I might perform one day. However, the theater was in a strip mall in between a convenience store and a hair salon—not exactly what I pictured. When I arrived, I drove back and forth, looking at the address to make sure it was the correct place. It was not what I was expecting. *How can magic happen here?* I thought. *And why on earth did someone recommend this place?* I walked in regardless: ready to learn, but terrified.

Gene

The acting coach welcomed students while setting up class. Intimidating, he reminded me of strict dance teachers and horseback riding coaches I had as a child, and they did not mince words. They had no qualms about letting you have it if you didn't do something correctly. All the students looked serious, beautiful, and of course, young. Next to the blonde bombshells, and dark, handsome men, I was out of my element. *The popular kids are taking over again*, I thought. *I don't fit in.* I sat in the back, observing—and praying the coach wouldn't call on me. Of course, he called on me (multiple times).

As the class progressed through the weeks, we completed many improvisations. I was having problems getting into my scenes, though. "Be in the moment, Heidi. Be in the moment. Be present with the person next to you," our director, Gene, would say frustratingly. "Read his feelings. Play off his emotions. Do you want to laugh, cry, flirt, yell? Let the feelings out Heidi." I hated it. I dreaded it. But I kept going and decided to take a comedy class, too.

This comedy class is where I learned how to better understand the way I come across to others. I learned the power of first impressions, how to own my look, and to let the audience know that you know what they think of you! For example, if you have a prominent facial feature, a strong personal style, or quirky personality, address it! It's the first impression an audience has of you, and the ability to laugh at yourself will help build a connection. At the time, it was challenging for me to recognize how I appeared to others, but in later years, when I developed my over-the-top Queen persona as part of my seminar personality, I also let the audience know, “I know what you are thinking. You see a little bit of a frustrated actress happening up here today, right?” The audience laughs. It's my warmup act. Instant rapport.

After the six-week comedy course, in 1989, I finally got my claim to fame. It was a Saturday morning, and on the radio, I heard a cattle-call for a position on the show *thirtysomething* as an extra. “Come on down to the convention center,” the radio personality screamed at me. “Be camera-ready.” At the time, *thirtysomething*, was an extremely popular TV show about—you guessed it—people in their 30s living in Philadelphia dealing with challenges of career and family. I heard a voice say, *Go!* So, I went.

The auditorium was filled with other young hopefuls. They gave us each a number, and one by one, they plucked us from our seats, terrified, and led us to a stage where we were instructed to walk, answer a couple questions, and have our photo taken. Hours passed as I anxiously waited for someone to call my name, to choose me. At last, an agent stepped on stage and announced to the group, “Don't call us, we’ll call you.”

I went home and then returned to my reality of running eating disorder groups. I knew I was making a difference in my job as a therapist, but fame of some sort was still calling my name. I felt powerful when on stage. Confident. Later that day, my phone rang. It was the casting director from *thirtysomething* saying they wanted me as part of their shoot that Friday. “Be on set at 5:30 a.m. for makeup, OK?” he said before hanging up.

I was elated. Prior to this, I only played a few small roles as an extra in extremely crowded scenes. I enjoyed the experience of getting to know the other "background cast members," as we were referred to, and seeing big-name Hollywood actors up close and personal. I once was in a movie with John Stamos and Gene Simmons of Kiss, *Never too Young to Die* (... it was the '80s). I was happy for the opportunity and excited to dive in!

As I drove to ABC studios at 5 a.m. that Friday, I felt like I had finally made it. I told the security guard my name, and he checked it off a list. *I was on a list!* I walked to the trailer for my hair and makeup, wondering where all the other extras were. This certainly didn't feel like the scenes I'd done previously. Once the makeup gal appeared, I asked her where everybody was. "Oh darling, it's just you," she said encouragingly. "You are the friend. The friend at the baby shower." My heart skipped a beat, a lump in my chest knotted. I didn't know what to do. Did I have lines to memorize? Did I miss something? Was it a mistake?

I walked on set and sat down in the living room I had watched so often on TV. Surreal. Even more surreal were all the actors in the show sitting around me. They were lovely, asked me questions, and welcomed me. My role was just to be *the friend,* but the words of my tough acting director, Gene, crept in. *Be present Heidi. Be in the moment Heidi. Play off the energy of the other actors,* I told myself. Even though I didn't have any lines, people would tune in and see me. I was going to be on a major TV network. My LA fantasies were coming true.

After this experience, the team at *thirtysomething* thought I would be a good fit as a stand-in (substitutes for the actor before filming) for Polly Draper, whose character was Ellyn Warren, a career politician with a rocky love life! I was tall and fit the bill. I said "yes" to the opportunity and went to the set a few times a week. This is where I got a behind-the-scenes experience. It was fun, but the love scenes were a bit daunting, even as a stand-in. I was frequently lying in the bed with a male stand-in, cameramen, and lighting crew dangling from the ceiling being directed to "Move your arm to the left Heidi. Lift your chin, Heidi. Move the sheets for lighting." I enjoyed the closeness to Hollywood, but I was taking time off work (calling in sick) to participate. This was, in part, because I didn't know until the night before if I was on the call sheet, and I knew my job wasn't thrilled with my acting project. I kept my mouth shut. I also didn't know if this was going to turn into something big or stay temporary.

I continued calling off work for a few more episodes when the *thirtysomething* crew asked me to stay on as Polly's stand-in. This would require me to cut my hair and dress like her. Basically, as her stand-in, I should look like her clone. There was still a little bit of an independent girl inside who thought, as attractive as she is, *I don't want to look like her. I don't want to cut my hair like her. I want to be me.* The compensation conversation came. What they were offering would not cover my bills and my modest apartment. I was torn. The crew encouraged me to take the risk. Who knows? "Many stand-ins and extras do become stars eventually," they persuaded me enthusiastically.

Despite having the confidence, charisma, and courage to jump into this new venture, my conservative values came into play. I wasn't willing to take the risk. I said *no*. It was hard, and I felt like I made a decision that might haunt me for the rest of my life. I was able to leave *thirtysomething* on good terms. I was invited to their Christmas party and said my goodbyes. The good news for me was that the show ended abruptly a few months later, and I realized I would have been completely out of a job and really struggling. Secretly, I was happy it ended.

Soon after, I took a break from acting and focused on my schooling and hospital position during the day.

I become immersed in my personal development journey. I started journal writing, taking dance movement classes, listening to motivational tapes, and taking women's empowerment workshops. As satisfyingly as my life was unfolding, I sensed a feeling of restlessness and started searching for a new profession in my field. Treating patients in a hospital with eating disorders was taxing, and I never saw the aftercare and recovery that many patients experienced. I didn't know if my patients were actually following the treatment plan that had been designed for them. So, I was left with an unsatisfied feeling with the results of our work together.

I found myself challenged once again with what was next. I applied to different hospitals seeking work as an in-house psychotherapist. After a lengthy talk, the woman interviewing me at one particular hospital said, “We don't have any positions presently open. However, I think you'd be great in marketing. We need an assistant to the marketing director.” She continued, “We'd love to have you on board.” I appreciated the opportunity, but, truthfully, I didn't really know what marketing meant. I was a therapist, not a businesswoman. This job was certainly not right for me. But they pursued me, apparently recognizing something I did not recognize in myself. What did they see? Confidence, charisma and courage? (And sparkle, of course!) Those skills are transferable to any position!

They said they would train me. I accepted the challenge. I took the position of marketing the therapeutic programs in their hospital setting.

I soon found that I loved marketing and business. It was creative, and that fit in surprisingly well with other marketing skills. I learned that marketing is about perfecting relationships. I learned professional networking skills, how to put events together with speakers, and how to market them to the community. It was a wonderful new experience where I was able to build my skill sets. However, there was tremendous pressure in the hospital community. In-house politics and pressure to admit patients as quickly as possible wore on me.

I just didn't know what I was supposed to do with my life. I would take my lunch breaks sitting in my car for a breather from the chaotic environment. I felt frustrated, lost, with no direction. I would use the rearview mirror to recite my affirmations, telling myself I am confident, I am good enough, I am capable of handling anything that comes my way.

One day, as I was sitting in my car, tears in my eyes, I decided to try my favorite self-love tool I learned from the acclaimed personal growth guru Louise Hay called "mirror work." (Yes, it's a real phrase.) Mirror work is about looking at yourself in the mirror without judgment and really looking into your eyes—your soul—as a way of connecting to yourself. I recall the first time I looked in the mirror and saw what was going on behind my eyes. I saw sadness. I cried. I saw a little girl who was afraid.

This particular day, in my car, I chose to really look into my eyes and to talk with myself, asking the harder questions. *What do you really want? What does your intuition say? Are you listening?* At that moment, I heard a voice. The voice said, *speaker services.* Around this time, I stumbled on a magazine where speakers listed their services for free as a marketing tool for their business. I never tried speaking publicly, but there was something about that magazine that pulled on my heart. I immediately called information to get the phone number for the organization.

Nichole

Nichole Carr, creator and founder, answered the phone. I blurted out, "I don't quite know why I'm calling you; however, I'm drawn to your magazine. Are you hiring? Looking for assistance?"

She said in such a matter-of-fact way, "Yes, we are. Let's meet."

My heart started pounding, and although I was not quite sure what was happening, I said, "I'll come right after work." I went back to the hospital after my lunch break with a little more bounce in my step.

Later that day, I met with Nichole. She lived in the heart of Venice Beach California in a little hideaway bungalow. She opened the door casually, as if we knew each other for years. She had *Mother Earth* written all over her. About ten years older than me, she wore a peasant skirt and no makeup, and her energy screamed hippy. I was hooked. I walked in with my corporate black and white pinstriped suit, tailored white blouse, heels, and a newly styled short haircut, but I felt no judgment. Little did I know, this was going to be a divine appointment.

Nichole guided me into a tiny nook where we sat to chat. There were candles lit and chimes gently singing in the background, creating a relaxed mood. Nichole, previously in the corporate publishing world, now worked out of her home. Clusters of high-end, professionally styled magazines were scattered everywhere. These, I learned, were the publications where she listed speakers with photos and bios, to build their business through public speaking. Surrounding us was a beehive of activity: a graphic artist interrupted us regarding a deadline, a couple of wayward-looking guys wandered about looking as though they'd just come in from the beach, several phone calls came through, a neighbor stopped by to drop off a key. This was a communal environment, certainly nothing I was accustomed to before, and I liked it.

Most impressively, Nichole remained focused on me, even with the chaos in the little bungalow (a good, stimulating chaos) and something told me this might be the beginning of a new chapter. Although the position in Nichole's business was not the right fit for me, she referred me to a professional women's networking group that she was involved with—truly a training ground for entrepreneurs. She told me that the founder and president, Barb Morelli, had a position open. Nichole believed it would be a perfect fit for me. The connection would change the direction of my life forever.

I learned they were looking for a marketing consultant for their networking group to sell memberships and advertising, so I interviewed with Barb, and she hired me on the spot. I felt at home in my new community and delighted in the networking events where hundreds of women entrepreneurs mixed, mingled, and supported one another's businesses. These were high-energy women. Risk takers in the big city. My type of women. I wondered how they made money. How did they risk a 9–5 income? How would it feel to have my own business?

At the time, I was content in my small cubicle making cold calls, following up with members, getting a steady paycheck, and attending stimulating meetings once or twice a month. There, I would observe the most popular women in attendance (just like I studied the popular kids in middle school). I wanted to understand what drew others to these women. Why were they desirable? I thought about how I was still shy and reserved—uncomfortable with myself prior to a meeting—while others gathered comfortably for presentations. Instead of hiding in the restroom prior to these events, I wanted to exude confidence. Simultaneously, I continued to find solace in my out-of-the-way cubicle.

The women at this networking organization became my inspiration. They networked flawlessly. Their presence made a statement. They conducted speaking engagements with confidence. They supported one another. Many had already published books. The realization dawned. I longed to be like them. One day I said to myself, *What happened, Heidi? You're great at sales. You have a master's in psychology. You've always wanted to be an actress. Do you want to spend another ten years in a cubicle, working on the phone? Somewhere, deep inside, there's another you longing to be seen and heard.*

My epiphany moment came when I recognized what I wanted but was unable to do it alone. I soon felt it was time to go to the next level with my newfound freedom. I was ready to create my own business and made the decision to combine my skills and become a business consultant and motivational speaker helping entrepreneurs, companies, and corporations build their business, increase their sales, and enhance their communication skills. I dove into my new career excitedly. I acted! First, I hired a public speaking coach and private coaches, and more speaking classes followed. I made an investment in myself, and I found that, ultimately, the greatest gift in investing in yourself is sharing your new gifts with others. And oh my, was I eager to share!

In six months, I had a full client load from referrals and speaking engagements from the Speaker Services magazine and face-to-face networking. My sisters Confidence, Charisma, and Courage were by my side. This was all prior to the internet. So I went out there and spoke for free one or two times a week to attract new clients, referred to as the "rubber chicken circuit." The rubber chicken circuit is a phrase coined by new speakers *paying their dues* and speaking for free. Often, the only compensation is the luncheon, which was usually rubbery chicken! However, this was part of the training, and I knew I was on my way to becoming a speaker, teacher, and coach empowering thousands of people to live more confident lives.

I grew to love LA. The networking, balancing a business, speaking, consulting—there wasn't any part of it that I didn't fully enjoy. It became the training ground for all I was to do and become in the future. Los Angeles gave me my confidence back. It's the city where I played a star; it's the city where I started my business. For those achievements, I will always be grateful.

Act II

Introducing: The Cast of Characters

Introducing – The Busy Bee

The Busy Bee is usually a hot mess. Others look at her and think, *How does she do it all?* And if you ask her how she gets it all done, frankly she won't be able to answer you. Why? Because she doesn't know herself. She's not that present and mindful of where she is and what is going on in her life.

The Busy Bee wears being late as a badge of honor but then wonders, *Where did the time go? What happened to my life? Didn't I always want to start a business? Have a family? A relationship? Travel? Get fit?*

The truth is busyness is another mask we wear that keeps us from playing bigger. It's easy to make light of the situation and say, "Oh, I'm a Busy Bee! That's just life!" But for a moment, let's take off the mask and dig into how this character might be keeping you stuck, small, and stressed.

We all want to feel empowered, right? Then what keeps us stuck? What keeps us from fulfilling our dreams and living a happier life? In my seminars, I ask, "How many of you feel like a talking head? So busy in your mind with thoughts and to-do lists that you feel separate from your body?" Everyone raises their hands. Everyone.

Busyness—I call it a disease. Because here's the thing: it is. And the disease of being busy is an affliction many of us carry, especially women. So many of us run around disconnected from our bodies. We are taking care of others, taking care of our careers, working on our personal growth, and relationships. In that respect, it's almost like an addiction, born out of trying to escape something. We don't want to look at our lives. We fear failure, yet mostly we fear success. When we are just *too busy,* it almost becomes an excuse. On the surface, it seems we are getting so much done, but there is a cost to our busyness. What happens? We crash. We get a cold and feel a bit under the weather, yet we keep plowing through. At some point, our body says, "Hey! I'm still here. I'm still important." (If you're reading this book, you know what I'm talking about). How many times a day do you hear yourself saying, "I can't fit it all in." or "I don't have time for me." That's the dreaded busy disease.

Let's be honest. Most of us are avoiding something when staying busy. We have a self-important agenda: "I'm so busy I couldn't possibly make time for that hobby, meditation, the kid's games, book club with the girls, date night with my partner, or keeping in touch with old friends." I like to call this response *dancing around the mulberry bush.* What we're really doing is stuffing our feelings. And what are those feelings? Usually fear, hurt, and pain. Often, we are just plain scared, and when we slow down to recognize and address these feelings, our vulnerabilities come to the surface. It takes our sister, Courage, to sit with those feelings, look at what's really going on, and take action to help heal what we've been avoiding.

I know I am in my busy disease when I walk out of the mall or grocery store and have no idea where I parked my car. I wander around the parking lot lost. I see folks in their car smiling at me, giving me that knowing look that says, *I've been there.* It's comical, but it's also a sign to me that I need to slow down. Where did I park? What route did I take to get here? Same thing when I can't find my keys, or if I find myself putting my cell phone in the refrigerator (which I've done). My head is leading, but my body is not following. It's scary when we realize our bodies are on autopilot and we've driven ourselves there unconsciously—sometimes we literally drive that way! We are living in a disease state, and as a result, our bodies and emotions are out of balance, and they have a way of eventually telling us.

In the past, my busy disease presented as pesky cold sores. I'd ignore them. I wouldn't slow down. I wouldn't listen to my body, and sure enough they'd get bigger. Feeling terribly, I'd slather on any and every available cream on the market. Nothing would help. Finally, I understood that it was my body telling me I was stressed. Don't get me wrong, it was good stress. I was networking, expanding my business, falling in love! But even good stress is stress, and overdoing anything can be taxing. Now, when I feel an inkling of a cold sore coming on, I stop, even when things are going well. I eat better. Get more sleep. Slow down. Exercise. Just generally take care of myself. It seems so simple, but when we're caught in the busy disease, we neglect our most basic needs. When this happens, I feel like Charisma is whispering to me to slow down, be present, and have more fun. I should have listened to her!

Then COVID-19 hit. Literally, the universe was forcing us to slow down, to be present, and yet many of us were also forced to quickly create or recreate ourselves, balance our families, career, work, and businesses ... all while trying to get comfortable in this horrifying new world. My Busy Bee took over center stage. *OK, Heidi, let's move quickly.* I thought. *I must go online 100% and change my in-person networking events to virtual.* I kept telling myself, in some ways, this has benefits. Confidence was by my side. I got this. I can create something bigger. But at what expense?

Exercise, eating, my daily morning rituals, reaching out to friends, and other pleasurable activities went out the window. I was glued to my computer learning a new form of technology, while pushing and pushing to market and inspire others to stay strong and find comfort in the presence of our group members. The good news, the business grew; the bad news, so did my waistline. I created a global network, but I felt overwhelmed. I gained weight, wasn't feeling good in my body, and received a diagnosis of arthritis in my hip. I was dumbfounded. How can this be? Isn't this an old lady disease? However, I realize age is nothing but a number! Yes, I'm 62 years old, but not 82. The body really does keep score. I'm not saying my busy disease is solely to blame for the arthritis brewing, but I do believe that ignoring the signs was a byproduct of the busy disease. I was checked-out from my body for an entire year. Like many of us, I knew I needed to navigate my new body and a pandemic world.

I wasn't alone though; I knew better! I teach this information, and like many others, I got off track. It was a wakeup call, or, as I like to say, a welcome call. I accepted this *new normal* realizing I needed to return to what I know works: asking for help, becoming more aware of my body's needs, mindfulness, taking time out for me. I'd wake up, and my body was reminding me, *Hello, I'm here. Please take care of me.* I embraced this calling and, as a result, felt back on track and living my best life.

As we get older, we tend to neglect the child within us. We lost the little girl who had big dreams. She played so effortlessly and creatively, manifesting her gifts at an age when she couldn't discern what was good, bad, right, or wrong. What happened to the little girl who felt free? Who would splash through puddles in the rain? Who said *no* and did not feel guilty about it? What happened to the confident, spontaneous, adventurous, creative, fun-loving child within? She got busy, that's all. She's taking care of others. She's taking care of a career, family, education, and life responsibilities. She forgot herself. She is now the Busy Bee. She cast herself in a role and others applauded her performance. Yet, performing on stage every day is wearing her down, and the audience is no longer invested. She's acting out her role, but the enthusiasm is gone. Unable to stop, she started dancing around the mulberry bush. She thinks her dreams are no longer important.

There's always time to change your mindset, and if you're reading this book right now, I believe your dreams are still alive, but perhaps stifled. It's time to confront the Busy Bee. It's time to stop, slow down, and breathe. Remove your mask. Let's see if another one emerges. Authentically. Unabashedly. Let's allow her to take center stage. She's raw. She's beautiful. She's empowered. Most importantly, she's you!

Let's look at the lessons we've learned from the Busy Bee and how taming her allows us to play bigger. The beautiful thing is that the sisters will be there to help you examine the stages of your life so you can see more clearly what's next for you.

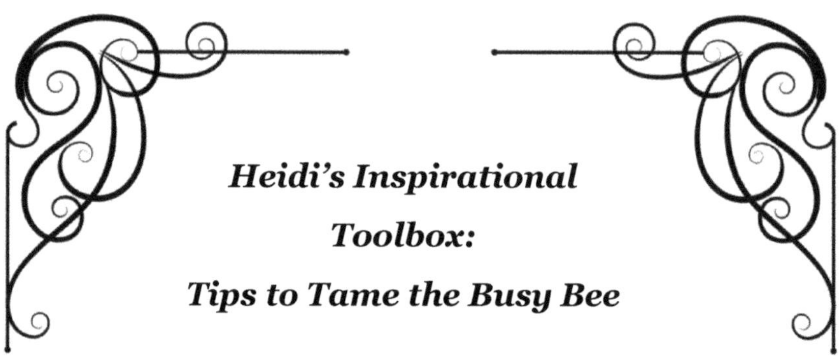

Heidi's Inspirational Toolbox: Tips to Tame the Busy Bee

- Assess what you can let go of to create space in your life and make time for what's important.
- Invest in yourself.
- Take time to listen to your body.
- Reconnect with your inner child and ask what she wanted for your life.
- Slow down, and breathe!

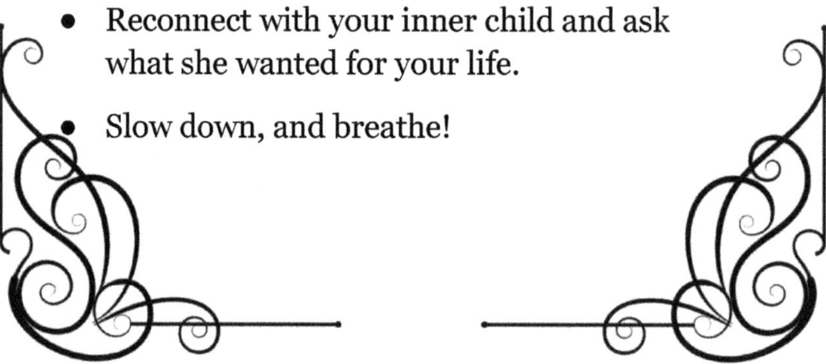

Introducing – The Feminine Woman

Feel feminine and "try on" something new

What does it mean to be a feminine woman? What I have learned along the way and now teach is that, when we come from our "feminine energy," it is our creative intuition. It's our inner wisdom. It's our heart. It's our spirituality. It's that whispering we hear that something is not quite right. It's that voice that says, "go for it" even though it may not make sense at the time. It's not the shoes, makeup, or clothing we wear (although appearance is an important component); it's about getting in touch with what feels good within, what makes you happy and peaceful. Femininity comes from the natural power of being comfortable with your essence: your inner, authentic self. You, as a woman!

When I'm truly listening to my inner being—my intuition, my feminine self—it will always let me know what I need to do next to feel more balanced. The issue is that we are not always the best listeners.

When I was living in Los Angeles, I experienced what I call my *masculine mode.* I was competing in business, negotiating contracts, and doing all of it alone. I became stressed, unhappy, depleted. In essence, I felt disconnected from my authentic self. I was beginning to reject my own femininity. During this time, I was also experiencing undiagnosable pelvic pain. I finally concluded that there might be a psychological link. Maybe the roles I had assumed—being the strong man fighting for myself and my business in a cruelly competitive market and unhappiness in my personal life —were affecting my health ... my feminine self.

Many of us have worked so hard to establish ourselves in a man's world that we often don't even realize our own feminine light is beginning to diminish. As women, we do have a masculine side, but the secret is not to allow it to become your dominant side. Don't lean into the busy disease by doing too much. I know it can be an ongoing challenge to find balance in our lives; however, if we don't listen to our inner knowing—our feminine energy and intuition—what happens? Yep, we crash. Masculine energy is the doing. Men go decisive shopping. Women, on the other hand, go window shopping (and it's easy to get off track when you're window shopping).

I was tired of dating. I kept getting involved in abusive and dead-end relationships. I felt a desperate need to feel, well, like a woman again. I was tired of paying for dinners, getting stood up, and having to take control of all my personal and business relationships. Working. Thinking. Doing. My life, in many ways, was transforming into a male mode of existing. *Desperate times call for desperate measures*, I thought. I listened to my body and my intuition, and heard, *Slow down, Heidi. Take a week with God*. To me, "a week with God" sounded like a resort. How lovely! I could do that, right? I could go on vacation by myself. Or could I? The reality was, I didn't have the budget for a getaway, and leaving felt complicated, adding more stress to my life. But I realized I could set up my own little week with God in my apartment instead of going to a fancy resort. I cleared my schedule and brought in the best people I could think of to help heal and organize my life. The folks who I knew could help me eat clean, relax, and encourage this special time I was going to create. I decided to take the plunge into the journey within. I felt giddy and guilty at the same time. In the end, I knew I was saving time, money, and energy. My soul was asking for this sacred space, and I was excited to go there. I put an out-of-town message on my answering machine and started my divine appointment.

I booked a couple sessions with a life coach during the week to help me dig into some of my questions about what was next for me. I saw a nutritionist who gave me a very complicated menu so I could do a cleanse and eat clean. Could I really do this? The ingredients and cooking seemed overwhelming; however, she referred me to a wonderful woman who brought me food daily and checked in on me. I was alone (but supported). Then I had a woman come to the house for a massage, a facial, and a body scrub. I went all out. I exercised daily, doing some aerobics, yoga, and walking on the beach. I spent time journal writing, digging deeper, discerning. Lastly, I wrote a letter to myself, to God, and to those I needed to forgive. This was a turning point in my life. The courage to go within is not for the weak. However, I knew the signs. I knew my masculine self was attacking my feminine self, and I knew I had to do something. I needed to create balance.

I felt so energized after this week. I felt renewed. I felt connected to God. I felt *high*. I felt open to receive what was next. And most importantly, I felt the healing of my body. My abnormal pap smears even went away.

I recently worked with a client who is the ultimate feminine beauty. She dresses exquisitely, she's always on point, always has a smile, and always spills charisma that could make you melt. She's confident in both her personal and professional life. However, there is something lacking inside. She's not spending enough time with her kids. She's not taking enough time for herself. She's working 14 hours a day. She's pushing the envelope, and logically, she knows it.

When I asked if this was a pattern from the past, she quickly acknowledged that to be the case. Believing we need to be in our masculine mode to succeed is what causes such stress in the first place. I asked her to take a couple of deep breaths and listen within for the answers. As quickly as I asked her, she blurted out what she knew she needed to do. "I need to let go of an employee I've been struggling with and get someone else to do my social media." But as soon as she said this out loud, she started backpedaling. "Oh, but I have to wait and see. Maybe the employee needs more training. If I could just be more disciplined on social media, I wouldn't be so burnt out. I'll wait and see, Heidi."

Of course, no judgment here, but can you relate? I have learned that our feminine answers don't always make logical sense. I believe this because I've tested it repeatedly—that the feminine way (with backup from our logical mind) is the answer to success.

We ended the session with a visualization: a quiet mediation about where she saw herself now and what she was going through. "I'm in quicksand. I just feel I'm sinking," she said. Impressed as always with her response and imagery, I validated her word picture. Then I asked her, "How can you get out?" Very simply she replied, "Heidi don't you know? You don't know how to get out of quicksand?" She paused and said, "You be still." Her mantra became *stand still.* Her soul, spirit, and intuition—or as I like to call it, "feminine energy"—was once again giving her the answer. I was happy to just facilitate the conversation.

Years later, when I formed my business, I decided I would only run it from my intuition, my feminine self. I didn't want to run it like my previous networking ways (where my fast-paced, pragmatic masculine brain ran out of control). Those days were gone.

I'd be lying, though, if I said that the feminine self is all about the inside, because it's not. Getting into your feminine also means looking at your outside self and how your outside self makes you feel. Too often, I witness women who neglect their outward appearance. They don't take time to do their hair, or they wear comfortable, yet unattractive, shoes and baggy clothes. These same women then wonder why they are unhappy with their professional and personal lives. They miss promotions at work and struggle with relationships at home.

The women who join my empowerment and networking group often give me pushback when this subject of getting into your feminine self comes up! *This is who I am, Heidi. I don't do red lipstick. I don't have time to get my hair done. I've never had a massage. Who cares what I wear? I just want to be comfortable.* It's a challenge I take on because I'm always amazed by the changes I see in one's confidence and charisma with some subtle new looks. I believe women *want* to feel beautiful, but often, we have just lost our way. We say, "Oh that's just for those young girls in their 20s and 30s." And I say, "It doesn't have to be." We can call on Courage to step out of our comfort zone and have some fun *trying on* new styles, new attitudes, and new ideas. Say *yes* to that little girl inside and encourage her to have fun, play dress up, and let her charisma and feminine self shine!

Addressing Dressing

Throughout my teenage and college years, I wore a very comfortable style of clothing: long skirts, jeans and T-shirts, sneakers. I did not have a strong sense of personal style, and I was unaware that my clothing reflected an impression of myself that wasn't authentic. This all changed when I stepped into my role at the networking organization. As I've mentioned, my networking world exploded. I was traveling the world yet looking—worse, feeling—utterly drab. However, I learned a lot about attire and appearance through this time of my life.

For instance, I remember, at one of my LA networking events, a lovely, beautiful woman named Lauren was getting frustrated by her networking efforts. Lauren was a yoga instructor, who offered retreats on *inner fitness*. She would attend these networking events in her cute yoga outfit showing off her toned body and basically projecting to the audience, *you can get fit like me if you take these classes.*

It backfired. Most of the women felt intimated by her physique, and it created a disconnect. Lauren shared, "I am doing everything right—attending meetings, supporting other members. Why am I not getting business?" My feedback to Lauren: her appearance was intimidating. "It's obvious that this is appropriate dress for you when you are the yoga instructor behind closed doors," I said. "But when you're here, you're out of place."

What she later learned is that when you show up at a networking event, you are the marketing person for your business. You must dress to attract the types of customers you like. Lauren was interested in getting into corporations and creating yoga and wellness programs. She took my advice to start dressing in a corporate style, and guess what happened? She possessed an entirely new energy. She was a businesswoman now, not just a yoga instructor. She looked powerful and confident. In turn, people treated her differently, and she started getting the respect she was looking for and referrals for corporate trainings.

Your looks might not matter to you, but they matter to other people. It's perhaps not the most flattering aspect of the human existence, but it's a part of life, nonetheless.

Another example of dressing for success comes from a businesswoman (the owner of four national franchises) who was one of my networking members. I always saw her in a T-shirt and jeans for as long as I'd known her. One day, over coffee, I asked her about what she felt her clothing was saying about her. She stated that she didn't want to stand out. She also didn't feel she measured up to the other successful women in the group. (Take a moment to let that sink in ... four national franchises, and she still feels like it's not enough.) When I suggested, as a homework assignment, that she wear a dress to our next meeting, she said she was scared. Although it was uncomfortable for her, she took the challenge to *try on* a different way of dressing. She contacted another friend for support. They went shopping and selected some clothing items appropriate for her body type and her daily living activities. A new hairstyle from a local salon. A make-up consult followed. Sensational!

She walked into our group with her new look. The women jumped up and down and surrounded her, gleefully dancing. “You look so beautiful. You are shining. Wow! Stunning and successful!” Here’s the thing. She had fun with all the attention and started walking and talking differently. She spent time and money on her new look, and it showed. She walked into a room and owned it.

With newly acquired public speaking skills, she shared her story with confidence and courage, inspiring the other women with her transformation and authenticity. I came to learn that she was the victim of an abusive relationship, thus perpetuating her low self-esteem. The simple act of changing up her look and allowing herself to be seen changed her life. I found myself looking to her as a role model. “Where’d you get that outfit?” I’d ask. With a smirk and a twinkle in her eye, she’d tell me about her latest skirt or accessory.

On the other end of the spectrum, another good friend of mine in my LA group was Sylvio. (Yes, we allowed men.) He was a carpet cleaner. I was always impressed with how he dressed when he attended our networking meetings. Polished from head to toe. Nice slacks, shiny shoes, and always a collared shirt. The first time I hired him to clean my carpets, I was surprised to see him dressed in ripped shorts with a white T-shirt and bandana around this head. That should be expected though, right? I saw no problem with that. He already knew *how to market a business to professionals by looking and dressing professionally* and then dressing appropriately to do your job. My point here is that sometimes addressing your dress is as easy as what

Sylvio did, but for women, it usually requires more of a financial investment and a time commitment.

Several years ago, we moved into a new home with a walk-in closet. Yes, my dream closet—color me ecstatic. Under the creative direction of a friend, Jennifer, a woman from one of my networking groups who was also a professional organizer, we created my very own shopping boutique. Before we started, she asked me an interesting question: "Who are your role models for dressing? Who do you think looks smart in their clothing? Who would you like to emulate?"

That was easy to answer. Two people came to mind. One was my friend herself, as she is always dressed impeccably: stylish, age-appropriate, yet with that sassy appeal that I love. I also mentioned another gal named Holly (also in my women's network group) who is known around town as the Fashion Diva. My friend pulled out each article of clothing, held it up and asked, "OK Heidi, would Holly or I wear this?" The answer 80% of the time was a big fat "no!"

As a professional woman, my clothing is important. Considerations: the audience I am addressing, my personal style, what makes me feel comfortable and confidant. What is age appropriate? I can be inspired by current fashion trends, but ultimately, I choose to build my wardrobe with clothes I love. Conservative. Formal. Fun. Funky (stilettos and leopard tucked in there somewhere). Add to that some statement jewelry, wrap-around stoles, and a variety of scarves. Shoes. Lots of shoes. I love dressing the part, and I encourage you to *try on* new roles and costumes to see how they make you feel. Do you walk differently, talk differently? Have fun with it. Play in your closet, and pretend it's show time!

It's cleansing to dig into your closet and let go of what doesn't work. I know there are so many areas in my life where I'm organized, yet my closet is not one of them. I have many emotions connected to my clothing. When I'm down and out, I've been known to binge shop (tops are my favorite). But I never really learned the art of pulling clothes together to coordinate, so, I'm often left with a one-shot wonder. I wear the top once or twice and get bored. Yikes, this cycle can go on and on. I've also attached clothing to my feelings about my weight. My weight continues to fluctuate, and it shows up in my closet. I tell myself, "Oh, keep those items, I'll fit into them again." The truth is, even when I have lost weight and was able to fit into them again, I didn't want those same clothes.

I remember another friend coming over prior to decluttering and walking through my closet. She very innocently commented, "Who needs ten pairs of black pants?" Well, apparently, I do. I have pants in there from sizes 10–16, even though the therapist and my personal growth self knew that was a dangerous set-up. It really was sabotage to keep all those sizes in the closet. On some level it made me feel as though I was never good enough—always being haunted by those size ten pants that hadn't fit for years—then remembering how uncomfortable I felt at a size 16.

I've learned to stay in the moment and change my closet regularly. I keep clothing color coordinated. I use the same hangers for everything. I only keep clothing that currently fits me. I sort my clothing per season. I'm more willing to let go of my clothes that don't fit or feel good and donate them. It's easier knowing someone else will get pleasure from my once-held treasures. I make my closet a fun boutique where I enjoy shopping. I even have a chandelier in there, a parting gift from Jennifer, my stylist and organizer. Everything is ready to wear. Clean. Pressed. Fresh. I adorn the shelves with my beautiful shoes, bags, and hats. Does my closet still sometimes outgrow itself after a few shopping splurges? Yes. However, I know now how to get back on track. And if I get lost in the weeds, my Jennifer is just a phone call away.

I believe that because of my theatrical background I like to see women try on new hairstyles, wear that sparkling scarf, or dare to put on a pair of red high heels. Something magical happens. Why are we so afraid? Is it judgment? That we won't be accepted? That we are out of our comfort zone? That's the point! I remember running one of my networking groups, and I gave one of the gals the homework assignment of coming to our next group wearing red lipstick. She wouldn't do it. It almost became a power struggle. I thought this was just a fun, safe way to play. She did not. The thought of wearing red lipstick and what it represented to her was, at first, too much. I've seen this before from others and accepted the push back; however, I did not want to give up. If she had this much resistance with this little exercise, truly something else must be brewing.

I gently reminded her that was why she was in the group, to practice in a safe environment, reaching out of her comfort zone. And why not try on this "prop" for fun? She did oblige and came to the next meeting with not only red lipstick on but heels and a fancy black dress. And you know what? She owned it. She walked differently and certainly had embraced the sisters Confidence, Charisma, and Courage. This exercise bolstered her feminine self and became a catalyst to exploring a part of her that she had hidden for so long. The spotlight was on her now, and she embraced it!

Trying new things—even just wearing a new outfit or style—helps us move outside our comfort zones and can help us feel empowered. It builds the confidence and courage muscles. For example, wear a style or color that is a little over the top (at least for you), layer several jewelry pieces for one outfit, or paint your nails red. Whatever you decide to do, make sure to add something new to your style and appearance that makes a statement. Have fun with it! Fashion should make you feel good.

The feminine answers are within each of us. We can truly heal ourselves when we listen. Otherwise, our body will tell us when we are tired, sick, burnt out, or have lost our direction; and if we don't listen the first time, the message usually just gets stronger and louder. The journey within to find your feminine self is a challenging one. It takes discipline. It takes time to get to know ourselves. When I do my daily disciplines to reignite my feminine self, I feel energized and inspired. They are my tools for practicing stillness. I light a candle, read an inspirational passage, mediate, pray, journal, and say my affirmations. I say out loud what I'm grateful for. Do I do this every day? No. However, when I do, I'm much more centered, healthy, and emotionally stable and handle my day with peace.

Heidi's Inspirational Toolbox:

Tips to Get into Your Powerful, Feminine Self

- Get out of your comfort zone. Visit a makeup counter and try on (and buy) a trendy, red lipstick or buy a pair of new red heels! Experiment. Play.
- Get clear on your style and what you want to project with it. First impressions count. What does the way you dress say about you?
- Get a friend or hire someone to help you clean out your closet.
- If you have a business, dress like the marketing person for your business. What do your clients want to see you dressed in?
- Light a candle. Focus on the flame. (Or visualize it if you aren't in front of one).
- Spend a week with you and your higher power or quiet self.
- Practice the daily disciplines: meditate, pray, or write in your journal.

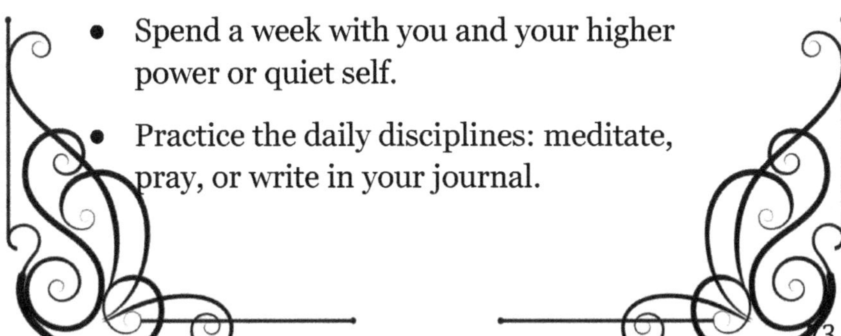

Introducing – The Drama Queen

Being a speaker satisfied a lot of my acting needs, but there was something about the smell of a small theater with grit and musk that made me really want to pursue it. I already dabbled in some TV shows like *thirtysomething* and enjoyed my time as an extra in a few movies. However, something else was calling my name. The small theater. Live theater. Scary but exciting!

The fantasy started when I was a child living in Staten Island, New York. My mother would take me into New York City to off-Broadway shows to experience creative theater and actors. I was enamored with the bright lights and overly opulent decor (even off-Broadway theaters looked elegant to me). The actors were glamorous, and I loved how much attention they received after their shows. I longed to speak on stage for an audience of my own. As an adult living in the world of glitz and glam, I wanted that experience even more. But now I wanted a 99-seat theater, and I wanted to do a one-woman show. Charisma grabbed my hand, and there was no turning back!

Caroline

Enter Caroline, a big-personality gal I met at one of my networking events. Caroline, together with her husband Nicholas, put together a 10-week acting course called Drama

Queens. I decided to join the program. During the course, we learned how to perform and utilize appropriate acting tools and techniques for theater. At the end of the course, we were supposed to perform a monologue in a showcase for our friends and family. It was supposed to resemble *Saturday Night Live*. It became clear early on, however, that I was the oddball once again. The girls were all perfect for the part. Pretty, in their 20s. This was the '90s, and they unabashedly talked about their latest diets and how they loved staying thin. I was never thin, and thought once again, *how can I perform with these women at my side?* My confidence gone, my charisma out of sight, I decided the only thing to do was call on Courage and stay, determined to do a fantastic job.

My piece was about a woman running late for an audition. "Hello, I'm here. I know I'm late," I begged. "I'll sing for you. I'll dance for you. Please wait." I begged like a fool complete with a giant, red curly wig. I sang poorly, danced like a clown, and walked away with great reviews. The best part was that I enjoyed it. I liked this! It was fun personal growth. The audience even said I was a good actress. I wondered, should I go back and pursue acting? Or just enjoy what it's bringing me right now?

The next class I took with Caroline was similar, except this time we were instructed to write our own one-woman monologue. This class required us to go deeper, bringing our mirror work into our performances. We wanted the audience to go on an emotional journey with us. We wanted to share our struggles and vulnerabilities: to show the audience our truth. I created a monologue called My Pink Coffin. A bit dark, admittedly. The scene started with me lying (dressed in black) in a box on the theater stage. There were no props, but we let the audience know this was my coffin. As I started talking about my coffin, and why I felt so helpless, I lifted my head to address the audience and let it be known, "The coffin is pink." This was met with laughter and applause. I also wore layers of clothing that represented different parts of my life.

As part of the skit, I screamed for help. I screamed twice because the actors who were supposed to run out the first time to help me missed their cue. "We are here. We are here," they finally snapped back in. Three of the gals came to me as I sat up and said, "I don't want this heavy necklace anymore as it represents my low self-esteem." They took it off me. "I don't want this sweater anymore as it represents the disappointments I've had with the men in my life and dating," I said. They took it off. Lastly, "Take off this blanket that is suffocating me and who I'm supposed to be," and they took it from me. It was cathartic. Even in this theatrical environment, it was a life-changing moment for me. I felt free. By letting myself shine in this environment, I was shedding the old me. A new journey was unfolding.

As my life continued to unfold, my theater background proved to be an asset in my quest to strengthen my skills as a motivational speaker and trainer.

When I returned to Erie years later, I created a community dance troupe called The Dancing Divas. We currently perform flash mobs with local bands and DJs. For many women, it is their first time performing. It takes confidence and charisma to learn how to *own the stage* and be a performer. However, after getting out of their comfort zones, and enjoying the accolades they received, the women blossomed in other areas of their lives as well. I also produced and acted in a play using the Drama Queen's script. I even included people who were new to acting to build their confidence. It was sold out every night. Caroline's husband, Nicholas, even traveled to Erie to support us and see our final show! A second play followed. Not so long after, my husband Phil and I were at a social gathering, and a gentleman, whose wife I'd worked with as her coach, asked why I enjoyed performing in community theater and flash mobs with my friends and colleagues so much. Phil, smiling, calmly responded, “She has to do them. It’s in her soul.” Yes. Listening to my inner voice does nourish my soul. Thank you, Phil!

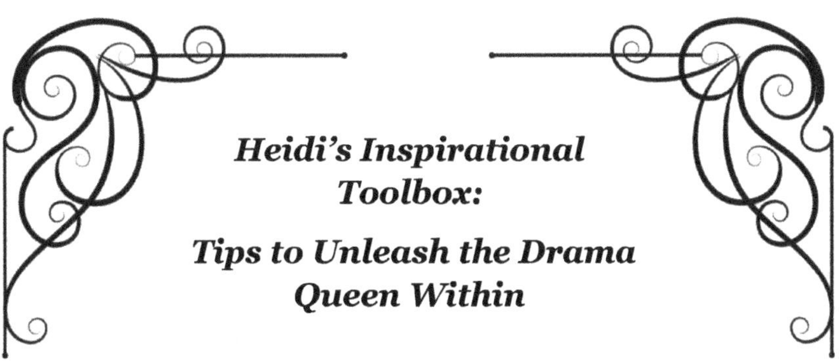

Heidi's Inspirational Toolbox:

Tips to Unleash the Drama Queen Within

- Take an acting, improvisational, or comedy class.
- Write your own monologue.
- Perform, even if it's just for yourself. Allow yourself to be seen. Push yourself further by joining a dance class.
- Remember to be vulnerable when you're creating.
- Transform yourself from who you are to who you want to be!

Every year my parents "produced" a nativity scene for our annual Christmas Card. The drama begins! 1967–1970

Professional portraits of Mom and Dad in Paris before getting married, 1958.

Mom and Dad on their wedding day, May 1959.

Living the L.A. life! My first modeling photo.

Moving into the ‘80s, still in L.A. awaiting my fame!

The punk era begins.

Hanging out with John Stamos on the set of the renowned film *Never Too Young To Die* in 1986. You didn't see it?

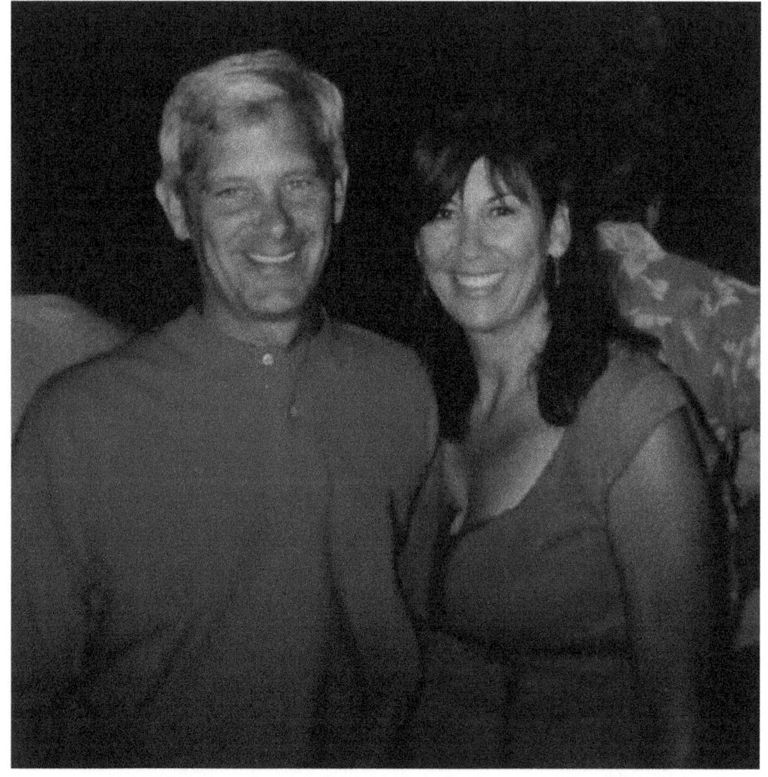

Meeting my future husband at my 25th high school reunion.

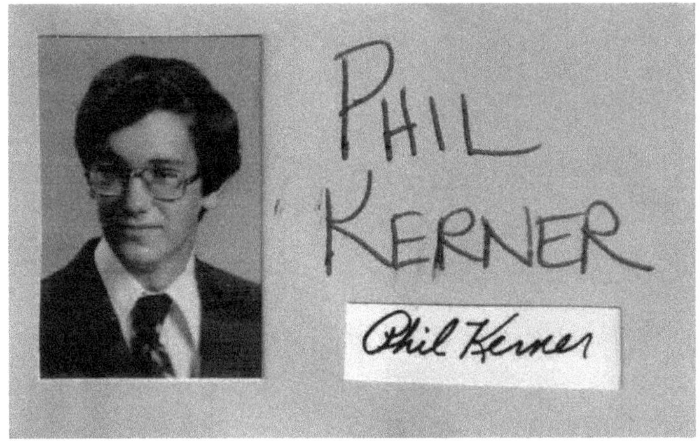

Our high school portraits... we apparently ran in different circles.

real women love and romance

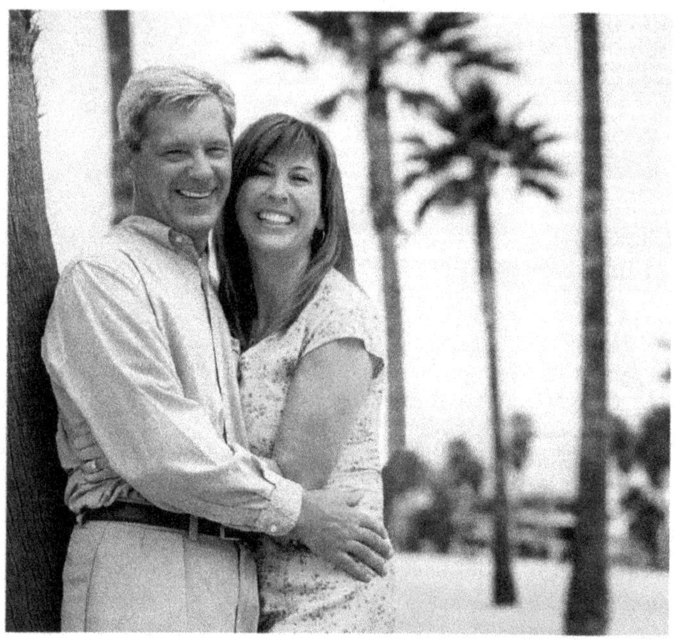

beauty and the geek

IN HIGH SCHOOL, HEIDI PARR AND PHIL KERNER TRAVELED IN DIFFERENT CIRCLES. THEIR WORLDS COLLIDED 25 YEARS LATER

If you wanted to make a movie about the love story of Heidi Parr and Phil Kerner, you'd probably cast Jennifer Garner and Mark Ruffalo as the leads. Twenty-five years ago, at McDowell High School in Erie, Pennsylvania, Heidi was the popular girl who dated jocks and Phil was a self-described geek who was so shy he never went on a date.

But lives change—and not always the way adolescents think they will. More often than not, geeks turn into handsome, successful guys and the prettiest girl in school never meets Mr. Right. That was the Heidi-Phil scenario in July 2003, when their high school class assembled for its 25th reunion. Heidi, who was living in California, had just about given up on love. Phil still

WRITTEN BY LUCHINA FISHER PHOTOGRAPH BY LISA ROMEREIN

Our love story was featured in *Lifetime Magazine for Women* in 2004. Written by Luchina Fisher, photograph by Lisa Romerein.

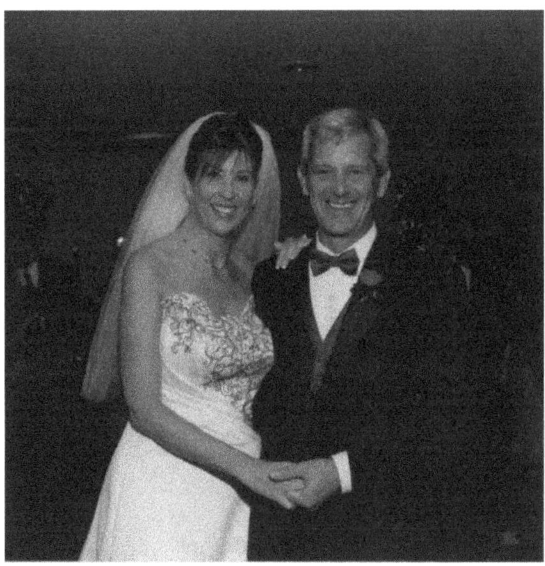

Our wedding day, October 23, 2004: the happiest day of my life!

My oldest stepson, Matthew, playing Green Day's *The Time of your Life* at our wedding.

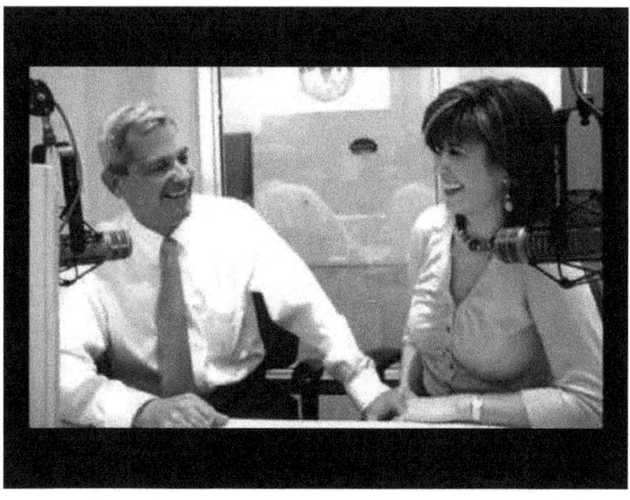

Hosting our own talk show, interviewing and supporting local business owners, on local AM radio WJET 1400.

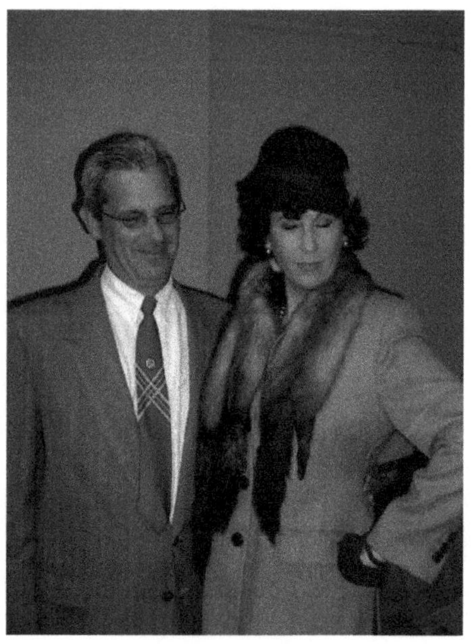

After moving back to Erie, of course I found the theater life. Phil and I were featured in the play, *The Petrified Forest*, directed by Michael Weiss

A dream come true: producing and acting in *Drama Queens* for a sold out crowd every night! Written by Jack Barnard

The Black Diamond Divas, my women's empowerment mastermind group, celebrates their graduation Hollywood style.

Dressed in white, the White Diamond Divas begin their journey to embracing their authentic selves.

I was chosen to be one of the celebrity contestants for the annual Catholic Charities Ball, 2013.

Gracing the cover of *Her Times* magazine, sharing my inspirational toolbox with a new audience, December 2, 2012.

Being recognized by the county executive for my dedication to empowering women and contributions to the Erie community, September 2015.

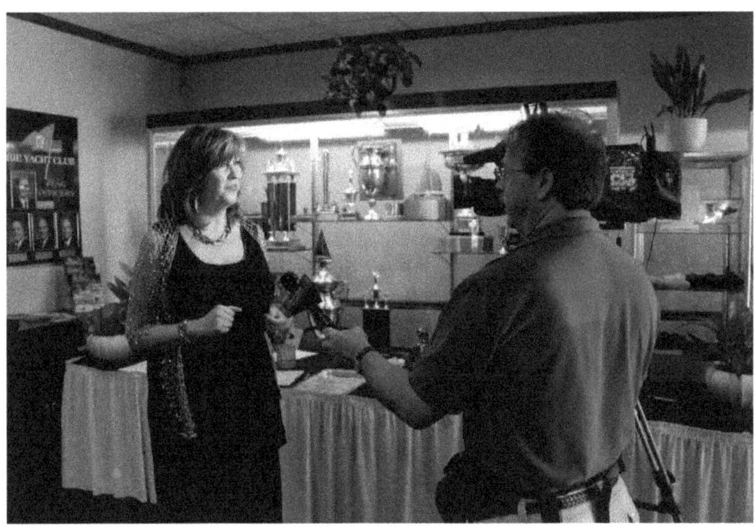

Meet the press: interviewing with the local television media for the book launch of *20 Lives Ignited*, August 2022.

Appearing regularly as a guest on local WJET TV 24, discussing women's issues and timely topics.

Striking a pose with my stepson Matthew (on the right) and his motorcycle buddies. Photo by Phil Kerner.

You're the one that I want! Dance routine playing Olivia Newton John for Parkinson Partners of Northwest PA charity event, 2019.

On the red carpet, celebrating another Coffee Club Divas anniversary.

Every year, I create my vision board. Marie Osmond continues to make her appearance as part of my inspiration!

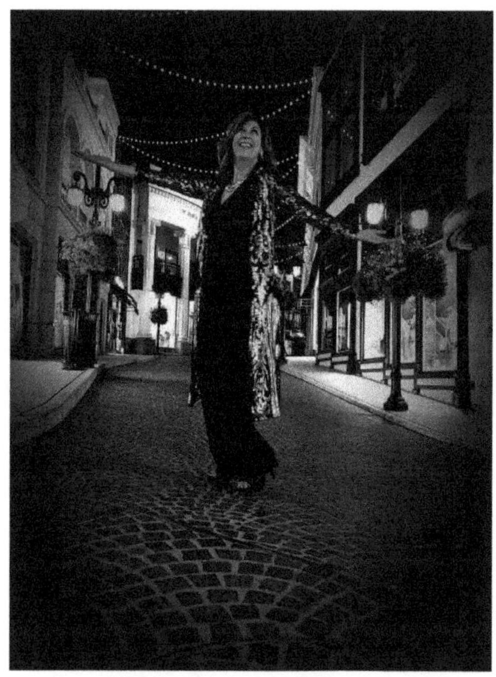

Nothing like visiting L.A. and posing on Rodeo Drive, 2020.

My sisters, my forever friends. They truly embody confidence, charisma, and courage.

We are family: a formal beach portrait of me with my five siblings and the woman who started it all. *Photo credit*: Paul Lorei Studios, 2021

Introducing – The Empowered Speaker

Whether you are speaking one on one, or on a stage, creating a video to be shared on social media or motivating your workplace team, it's essential that you bring in the sisters Confidence, Charisma, and Courage to help you deliver your message clearly.

I loved my job at the women's networking group, in part, because I regularly attended huge networking events and it kept me inspired. It was required for me to attend as we were always looking for new members and because it was good customer service. During the day though, I was stuffed away in a tiny cubicle inside the main office, selling memberships and advertising. I was new to sales, but I had the psychology of people down. I learned marketing skills and event planning from my hospital experience. *But sales? Selling over the phone?* Intimidating and scary, psychology background or not.

Barb

Barb taught me that sales was about connecting confidence with charisma, and if you've ever done this work, you know it takes courage to ask for a sale! When I first learned the art of selling, I hated it. My shyness took over. I was intimated by the phone. I didn't know how to sell and talk about numbers and discounts. Even though I had a script, people just hung up on me.

Oh, what am I going to do? I thought. I need this job. I need to learn how to sell these memberships! I would go home and cry. Where were my sisters? Confidence, Charisma, and Courage were nowhere to be found ... or so I thought.

Barb would tape my phone calls (which was legal back then) so she could listen to my tone of voice and my word choices. The purpose was to detect what I was doing—or not doing—correctly that was impacting my sales.

She was excited to discover the culprit. “I know why nobody is buying from you, Heidi. You have the puppy dog syndrome.”

I had *no* idea what that meant, but I quickly learned the meaning of the phrase.

“Heidi, you are too excited when you talk to people on the phone. You sound like an anxious and overly excited puppy dog. Your enthusiasm might be authentic; however, it's not translating to the potential member over the phone. They don't trust you. Your voice gets high and comes across salesy.”

“But that's me,” I pleaded with Barb. “I so believe in this amazing networking group. I see the results these women are getting by networking. How can I not be jumping for joy?”

"That may be how you feel, Heidi, but you are not reading your potential customer. You must deliver and share the information in the way that the customer needs to hear it and believe it.”

“How do I do that Barb? How do I change my tone of voice?”

Barb patiently coached me in how to lower my voice at end of each sentence and to use the power of the pause, which is a presentation tool meaning to speak slowly and be present when you talk. It helps build trust. Many women end our sentences as a question instead of a statement, with our voice getting higher at the end, just like when you ask a question.

I literally would lean over my desk and rest my head on my elbow, *slow down, Heidi, don't get too excited. I can share the same information with potential customers by simply adjusting my delivery.* Watch your tone. And end your sentences as a statement. Not a question! And guess what happened? One membership after another, sold, sold, and SOLD. The bell would ring each time I got off the call with credit card number in hand. No longer was I a puppy dog.

I didn't realize it at the time, but Barb was showing me how to use my charisma in a new way. Charisma knows how to connect with people. She listens and puts her own agenda away. I had a new-found confidence as well.. Within eight months I was the top salesperson at the company. It took courage to take the coaching to heart and keep picking up that phone even though I was getting rejected.

Now that I was doing well in sales, Barb challenged me to step up my game by asking me to start making announcements at our networking events. This petrified me. Remember, I wasn't a public speaker yet! Public speaking wasn't even in my tool shed.

Barb started me off small and created a specific script for me that included our mission statement, how the group started, and upcoming events and announcements. All I was required to do was read it; however, getting up in front of 100 women terrified me (preplanned script or not!). I would obsess over the words before going up, shaking in fear, and afterward, I always felt I presented poorly.

Barb, though, was not a woman who minced words. She validated my poor performance with, "Heidi, I know you always get nervous, but you don't even sound like you. Your voice. Your presence. It's like you've become someone else."

To me, Barb was larger than life. Her personality was no fluff, direct, with a "do it my way" attitude. It was easy for Barb to stay present and to be herself because she knew who she was and owned it. She is brilliant and confident, but also reserved and not one to readily smile. She is the blunt, strong-minded woman you wanted in your corner. In fact, I now call Barb a friend and forever mentor.

I explained to her that my nervousness was completely out of my control.

"That is because you are narcissistic," she said.

I stared at her, amazed she had the nerve to say something like this to someone else in total seriousness. "What?" I said, "How can you say that? I'm a deeply caring person. I think of others first."

"What I mean," she said, "is that you are so busy thinking about the audience, and what they're thinking about you, that you are not present to them or for them. You are making it about you."

Tears welled in my eyes. "Let me think about what you're saying," I replied sheepishly, hurt feelings intact. I took a deep breath.

Of course, she was right. Barb was always right. I was so worried about how I looked: was my lipstick on correctly? Was my outfit appropriate? Was I mispronouncing something? On and on and on in my head I could go. I knew a few tricks from my coaching and speaking classes about transitions, how to carry myself, and even breathing exercises, but what Barb was proposing was a new psychological aspect I never considered. Good public speaking wasn't about me. It was about my audience. Wow, what a concept!

Once I absorbed Barb's words (not easily) and learned to apply them, I became more comfortable and confident in front of these groups. Many of these networkers even became my friends. I started letting my true personality come out from time to time. I laughed at myself, and guess what? I didn't die. In fact, the audience would even laugh with me most of the time. I started using the power of the pause while doing improvisations and asking audience members to add their two cents to some of my comments.

"Who's taken this seminar before and would like to share?" I'd ask. "What's your number one secret to being a good networker? Who has a testimonial from another member you'd like to give a shout-out to?"

Barb's mindset message changed how I dealt with audiences forever. It's not about me, and if I'm nervous, I'm probably making it about me. Being a speaker and having a message that shares your education, point of view, or your products or services is a gift. Whenever I conduct a speaking engagement and still feel *the jitters* before addressing my audience, I pause a moment, take a breath, and let go of me. This is about them. How can I serve them? How can I deliver this message in the best way possible so they understand my points?

Now don't get me wrong, I practice. I never wing it. I don't memorize the material (a big no-no!), but I now allow my intuition, and my message, to take over. I have prepared for this presentation. I trust the audience is meant to be with me and to hear the information I have to share.

As the meeting continued, I started going off-script and getting a little more creative, bonding with my audience, and enjoying it. To my chagrin, however, I started seeing little red marks scribbled on my next script stating: "Heidi, please stick to the script. Don't forget the important line you left out last time." *Uh oh,* I thought. I was getting comfortable with speaking, yet I felt the chains around me tightening. Barb was setting a boundary and giving me a stop sign. It was heard, but I felt like a rebellious teenager wanting to do it my way. Confidence emerged again, and I didn't want her to disappear. I knew it was time for my next steps, and I was getting ready.

I started building my consulting business, helping entrepreneurs market themselves and speak to companies about communication skills. During this time, I was introduced to a company that hired speakers to conduct all-day seminars for their companies and corporations on professional development. This job required me to be on the road 100% of the time. I was traveling from one city to the next, using their templates as a guideline yet delivering the material with my background, personality, and creativity. They would train us, but ultimately, they wanted to hire speakers who were already polished and ready to go. There was an audition process in Kansas City and, sure enough, I got the part! They handed me a ticket to travel to Hawaii the following week.

I refer to this time in my life as an internship. This is prior to 9/11, so travel was easy, but simply lugging myself from city to city was exhausting (and I was young!). Once again that voice inside said, *You would never have traveled to these places on your own. Learn. Practice. Get comfortable with being uncomfortable.* I was on the road for the next two years. They flew me home to Los Angeles every Friday night, and I left every Sunday afternoon for the next journey. As they say, being on the road isn't as glamorous as you think it would be. Many times, I would be in an exciting city but not have time to explore any part of it other than the confines of my hotel room and a banquet hall.

My smallest audience included 100 people. Often it was a mixture of employees from the janitor to the CEO. The funny part was that most of the audience didn't even want me there. This was not a seminar they chose; this was a seminar they were mandated to attend. Walking into a room full of folks that don't want to be there takes some bells and whistles, fancy footwork, and the sisters by my side!

My first step was to *work the room* and to meet every single person as they were getting settled in. It builds rapport and sets the stage, so you are warmed up to your audience (and they are to you as well). "What's your position in the company? What would you like to get out of today? Wow, what great earrings, where did you get them?" were my go-to ice breakers.

It was my job to transform my nervous energy into enthusiasm. I could see in their body language with crossed arms and disinterested looks that they did not want to be there. I addressed the elephant in the room.

Once I took the stage, I let it be known: "I know some of you are thinking, what is this Los Angeles fancy pants girl going to teach me?" Immediately I saw them soften. That's what they were thinking. I let them know that I understood, and it was OK to *not* want to be there; however, my challenge to them was as follows: "We are here all day together. Let's take advantage of this time. Let's see if we can be open to learning a new way of dealing with stress, difficult people, public speaking, or whatever the topic is for the day." I had my inside affirmations going: *Be present, Heidi. Get them to buy into you, Heidi. Make them laugh, Heidi. Make it fun. Be inspirational.* And I did. They were still tough. But I had Confidence, Charisma, and Courage on my side, and they got me through each speaking engagement.

After each seminar, I collected the evaluations. It was like my own report card, and the critics were cruel. Why on earth the company trusted us to send our bad evaluations back is something I will never understand. I know many of my fellow seminar leaders threw out any evaluations with unflattering comments. Not me. The good news was they were always 90% great! They had to be, as the company expected those scores to keep us in good standing.

However, the one to two evaluations that were critical devastated me. I would eat my dinner in my hotel room and read and reread the negative comments. "Heidi is a Pollyanna. Heidi's hair is a mess. Heidi thinks she's too good for us being from Los Angeles." I eventually told audiences I was from Erie. The tears would come. And then I remembered my mirror work, my affirmations, and the self-esteem work (the same things I was teaching my attendees but not always practicing myself). It helped but was a process. I just continued to do the best I could do. I honed my craft. I read books written by comedians on how to deal with hecklers since I could never come up with a good comeback line. (The worst thing you could do is have a *deer caught in the headlights* look.)

The job was overall a wonderful experience, though. It took me to several places where I made sure I stayed for a few extra days so I could explore these amazing cities and countries. Once, when I was speaking in England and conducting a women's communication seminar, I had the sense it would be a trip of a lifetime, and it was. I asked all of them to stand and mix and mingle. As per my trainings, I always started with an icebreaker to get the audience comfortable. For the first time, the audience didn't move. I asked again, and they just sat there.

Finally, one of the women blurted out, "Heidi, you do know we are English, don't you? We don't do things like that."

Impishly, and with a little twinkle in my eyes—armed with my best friend, Confidence—I said authoritatively, "I know you are English, and today you have an American seminar leader, and we are going to do things my way."

They put their heads down, giggled, got up, and responded as instructed.

Texas, Alaska, Idaho, Scotland, Hawaii, New York, and on I went. To this day, whenever I complete a corporate training on communication skills or various professional development topics, I quietly say to myself on the way home, *Thank you for my internship being on the road. Thank you for my tough audiences. Thank you for my training, so I can make a living now and help my audience members increase their confidence, charisma, and of course, courage!*

Heidi's Inspirational Toolbox:

How to Speak with Confidence

Transform your nervous energy into enthusiasm!

- Arrive early for any type of event you might be in charge of to meet and greet each person attending. You can do this virtually, too!
- Make it about the audience and the people attending your event—not you! Don't worry about what you look or sound like, but focus on the message you're giving to others.
- Personalize your speech or presentation. Don't be afraid to use analogies or tell a brief story about yourself. Add some humor!
- Use the power of the pause. Try to remember to slow down and be present.
- Maintain eye contact.
- Hire a speech coach if you are doing presentations on a regular basis.
- Practice, practice, practice!

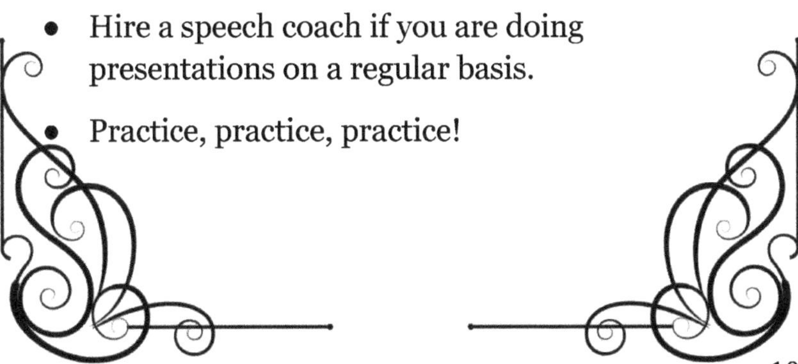

Introducing – The Networking Queen

Working within the women's networking group made it clear: women who network succeeded. We, because at this point I was one of those women, weren't aggressive in our networking approaches; there was no business card shoving.

I learned a lot from networking, but the biggest lesson was that I needed Confidence, Charisma, and Courage at my side when I was entering any environment where I met new people, from networking to connecting with neighbors to standing in line waiting on an order.

Networking is *work*, so if one goes just *hoping something will happen* it usually doesn't. We were taught to go to networking meetings with a purpose—to have a goal in mind. The same should follow for really any place you go with any new people you are approaching. Are you trying to find a job? Looking for a group of like-minded professionals? Discovering new friends? Selling a product or service? Searching for a mentor? Promoting a book?

We learned we needed to get to know one another, build relationships, and understand potential connections: you don't know who knows whom or where your next connection might come from. It's important to treat each person with respect. We learned it's about giving first and not expecting something in return. In my time speaking, traveling, and networking, I learned my networking process is simple: (1) have the courage to work the room with confidence and charisma and (2) get your chat on. You got it: It's the same for any new group of people you want to connect with.

In my seminars, I like to refer to myself as a recovering introvert. I still have introverted tendencies, but I learned how to stick out my hand and say *hello*. You will appear more confident, composed, comfortable, and professional in networking situations if you plan ahead, attend every meeting, arrive early, settle in before the meeting commences, and use the restroom prior to the event. Being prepared sets you up for easy conversation: 90% of success is in just showing up, seriously. If you're prepared, and show up, you're going to—at the very least—have a decent time. It's sort of like working out. You may not feel like it or have 100 excuses why you don't need to do it, but when you do, you feel fabulous! Every time I attend a networking event, I'm inspired, I meet new people, and I'm reenergized about my business.

Getting your chat on is also about making small talk feel comfortable. What happens when you walk into the room and don't see anyone you know? Do you run and hide at the buffet table? Sit down and look busy on your phone? Or take refuge in the restroom like I used to do? No. You find someone new—and this is the trick—you ask questions, and then you keep your mouth shut. That's right! Keeping your mouth (mostly) shut is the key to great conversation. People love to talk about themselves once you get them started. Confident people ask questions and interview others; this puts you in the driver's seat.

Working the room with confidence is key. Many of my clients *freak out* walking into a room where they don't know anyone. So, it's time to bring in Sister Charisma, who is going to build new relationships with a smile and Sister Courage who's going to take a deep breath and help us walk into the room and own it with Sister Confidence!

I know, I know— you hate small talk. You think it's boring and want to just get to the meat of the situation. I remind my clients that small talk is part of the process, and once you embrace this conversational tool, you will open up a new world of connections.

Let me show you how.

Start with a smile. Make sure to start smiling *before* you ever walk in the room. Get to the event early and ask Charisma to help you shine!

With Confidence, Charisma, and Courage at your side, approach someone you notice is alone and say*, hello*. Yes, this works for non-networking events too. Ask questions.

- *Hello, my name is Heidi. What's yours?*
- *I haven't been to this type of event before. How did you hear about this?*
- *What a wonderful bright blouse you have on. I love the color yellow. Where did you get it?*
- *Beautiful day, isn't it?* Don't be afraid to talk about the weather. Everyone has something to say about it, and it breaks the ice.

Charisma knows people love to talk about themselves, so find some common ground.

When you don't have a warm-up act and you go right for the "what do you do" question, it will sound like this:

Me: *What do you do for a living?*

Other person: *I'm an attorney.*

Me: *Oh nice, what is your specialty?*

Other person: *Family law.*

Me: *So how long have you been practicing?*

Other person: *Ten years.*

Get the picture? So frustrating. I'm asking questions with one-word answers and missing the opportunity to make them feel comfortable before going deeper. Remember, we want to bring our sister Charisma in here. Be engaging.

I have a rule: *no sitting down until the meeting starts.* Charisma reminds us that first impressions count. Remember your body language says more about you than what you actually say.

Many folks have a challenge saying goodbye, but it's OK to disengage after opening up the conversation.

Here are some pointers:

- *It was nice meeting you. I need to say hello to a few more people before the meeting starts.*
- *Would you give me your business card? It would be great to stay in touch.*
- *Oh, I see Rebecca over there. I'd love for you to meet her.* (Link people up!)

Your confidence will soar with these small talk conversation openers. You never know how one person might be connected to someone else, even leading you to your next client, referral, or friend! Have fun with it, and make sure to follow up with these new contacts within 24 hours so the acquaintance remembers you. Even if you're meeting new people at a non-work event, it's nice to send a text or Facebook message just to let them know you remember them and enjoyed the interaction.

Whether you are the CEO of a company, an entrepreneur, working for someone else, or working in a nonprofit or at a university, networking skills are the key to your success. People do business with people they know, like, and trust. If you connect with others, help them feel good about themselves, and carry on a conversation with confidence, you are 80% closer to becoming more successful in any business or work environment, as well as in your social life.

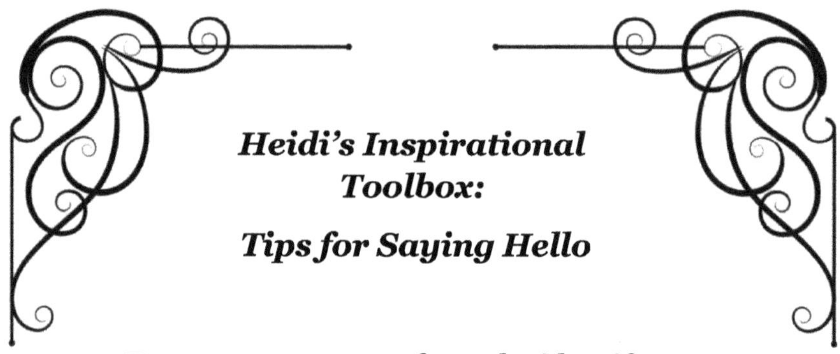

Heidi's Inspirational Toolbox:

Tips for Saying Hello

- For any new group of people, identify your goal. Get clear on your purpose for being there so you will be successful.
- Walk into a room and smile. Be confident, and work the room before taking your seat.
- After you initiate conversation, ask open-ended questions so you don't illicit boring, one-word responses.
- Find the common ground between you and your audience and use it to your advantage.
- Follow up with the leads you create and connections you want to maintain for ongoing connections, collaborations, and clients.

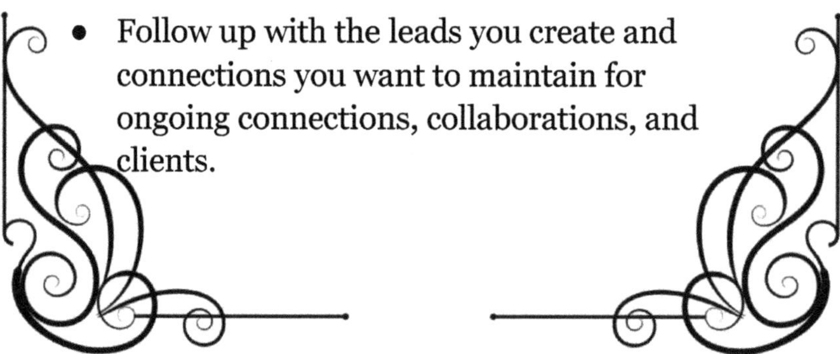

Introducing – The Tardy Ts

I'm often surprised that time management is one of my most sought-after topics in both the entrepreneurial world and with my corporate clients. Many of my clients have shared with me that they struggle with a lack of discipline. They're unable to get basic tasks done, don't know how to prioritize, have problems with chronic procrastination, and have endless excuses preventing them from improvement.

I understand we are all busy and over-scheduled, but we can improve this mindset. I often hear, "I couldn't get her off the phone. She kept talking." I also hear, "I'm so overbooked, I just didn't know how to say *no*." Let's look at how time management plays out in our inner and outer world, and how you can become inspired to gain control of your life. At the end of the day, it doesn't matter how confident or charismatic you are, if you constantly show up late, people aren't going to take you seriously.

I believe that being on time really comes down to two words: respect and discipline. Repeatedly, I see how people's inability to be on time affects them in negative ways, especially in their social and professional circles. First impressions matter, and if you're showing up late, that's the first thing people are going to notice about you, not your nice eyes or smile. Beyond first impressions, if you observe someone who is always late, you might really begin to wonder: How do they manage other areas of their life? Are they always unprofessional? Are they seeking attention? The point is, your friends, family, and coworkers do not know why you're arriving late—they just know you're late, and this sends a lot of mixed signals to the people around you.

Tina

My dear, forever friend Tina was always late for everything. I'm not talking about a few minutes late; I'm saying hours and hours late. As a former therapist, I tend to label this behavior as passive aggressive: calling to say she was on her way, then calling again with another excuse. "Just another ten minutes," she'd say, and on it went. It frustrated me. I felt disrespected. Tina is one of the most creative entrepreneurs I know. As a hairdresser and salon owner, she is so creative with her craft and how she presents herself: her hair is always cutting edge and on point. She travels to New York City on a regular basis to keep up with trends. Her clothing is a mix of vintage style and '80s punk, and she loves thrift shopping. Nothing ever matches, but it works. She has internal leadership skills that make people want to follow her. Including me.

Ever the socializer, she never has an empty apartment or house. There is always family around—a lot of family. She's Italian and Catholic, I remind myself with a smile. Even to this day, I love visiting Tina. Whenever I walk into her home, I feel like I'm transported into the movie *My Big Fat Greek Wedding*. Every corner of her home has a statue of the Virgin Mary, Jesus on the cross, or a rosary. People and food are everywhere. I refer to the ever-changing ensemble of people in her life as *Tina's Troupe of Broken Birds*. It's a wonderful quality of hers: she is always giving comfort and support to those who are down and out.

I went to high school with Tina, but we didn't hang out as friends. However, when I moved home from Ithaca College to Erie for two years in 1982, and before moving to Los Angeles, I was referred to her by a mutual friend to get my hair done. Tina was a wonderful and creative hairdresser. I started going to her, and we became fast friends.

Tina and her sister created fashion shows that were performed around town, and I soon joined in those. We dressed in vintage-style clothing, sporting razor-sharp punk hair styles and highly sprayed hairdos that looked like cones molded to our heads. So fun. So fabulous. All the gals were tiny and waif-like, and so were the dresses.

There was much laughter in the dressing rooms before a fashion show when it took a couple of the gals to squeeze me into the vintage dresses. They were the sophisticated models working the runway with glamour. Conversely, I came out of the gate with black cat eyeglasses, chewing gum, and performing just a little over the top, for comic relief. So fun! Our troupe modeled in Erie and Pittsburgh. However, there was a problem with our amazing ringleader, Tina. You guessed it, she was always late.

Whether it was for a fashion show, party, theatrical or social gathering, fundraiser, or dance recital, it didn't matter what she invited us to attend, we were there on time ... and Tina wasn't. People would be waiting for the show to begin, and she'd be nowhere in sight. Naturally, when she finally appeared, everyone was outraged. She would walk in and apologize—and I can still see to this day—everyone literally turned their backs on her, fed up with the lack of respect.

Her tardiness was so strange to us because she has such a warm heart, she's a loyal friend, and is a brilliant and creative entrepreneur with big ambitions. Why couldn't she get this right? The therapist and friend in me sat her down one day and asked her a pertinent yet curious question. "Tina, why is it when you walk into an event, you have set it up so everyone is angry at you? Why don't you *want* to walk into a room and have everyone overjoyed to see you?" I really dug in, asking her some hard questions. "Where did this come from? How does it make you feel?" I pressed. "Do you not feel you deserve acceptance? Love?"

I knew she was not trying to annoy or disrespect us on purpose. She admitted, "I don't know. I feel so badly and guilty. I never thought of it that way. Is my self-esteem so low that I create big events knowing I'll fail? I don't want people to be angry with me." I saw a light in her eyes as she seemed to look at it from a different perspective. She asked herself right in front of me, "Why do I want people angry at me? I hate it, but I can see how I set myself up!" Something happened that day. Tina made an inner decision that she wanted smiles and love when she walked into a room *because she deserved it.* As a result, Tina is now always on time!

Trish

Once or twice a year, I host an intimate women's empowerment group. This particular year, 12 professional women committed to a six-month period of meeting in person. They gathered twice a month to work on their communication skills and building their businesses. At the first meeting, I clearly identified the rules, which included being on time. To me, that meant arriving early to get settled in, having a cup of coffee, and greeting the other women. The problem was that one of our members, Trish, was chronically late.

Trish, always aflutter, would share her plight and apologies while making her grand entrance. "I'm so sorry. I had an order. I had a customer. My car broke down." It was always something, and she tried to make a good case. The members, empathetic, would abruptly stop everything in our group process, hug her with understanding, and warmly welcome her into the circle. It happened again. And then again. I knew as a good seminar leader and former therapist, that a codependency was developing, and we needed to address this issue. It was uncomfortable and disruptive to the entire group, and it especially bothered me.

As we do in these intimate intense groups, we addressed the issue. If one area in our lives is not working, it affects all areas of our lives. When we asked curious questions to Trish about her chronic lateness, she admitted it was a problem. However, she always had a reason and spent quite a bit of time trying to persuade the rest of us to accept *why* she was late. My concern, and what I didn't hear, was her taking responsibility.

"Is this behavior affecting your business?" I asked.

Sheepishly she replied, "Yes."

Sometimes drastic behavior needs to be interrupted in a dramatic way. As I've mentioned, I often use theater tools and role-playing to truly heal one's issues. When talk therapy doesn't work, let's *act it out*, as I say. So, I decided to be a bit more proactive in my coaching of Trish. Now, I needed to get the other members to *buy into* my suggestion.

At the next meeting—prior to Trish's anticipated grand entrance—I advised the members to *not* look at her when she came in as some have in the past. I didn't want us to stop the group process just for her. They expressed concern. They were nervous. "Heidi ... that's mean," they said. "She can't help it." We discussed further and concluded that we were enabling her to act in this distracting way by allowing her to keep showing up late without consequences. I stressed the importance of making it stop. Understandably, the women were conflicted, nervous. They felt they were being mean, insensitive to Trish's needs.

Fifteen minutes later, as we were going around the room concluding the first portion of the meeting, the door flies open. Trish arrives, breathless as always. Nobody looks up. We keep on with the meeting. It was very uncomfortable for all of us, yet I wanted to trust the process. Trish looked around the room. Her disappointment and confusion were palpable. Slowly she moved to the couch, sat back, crossed her leg. She looked at me and stuck her tongue out like a nine-year-old child. Message received. Trish was never late again.

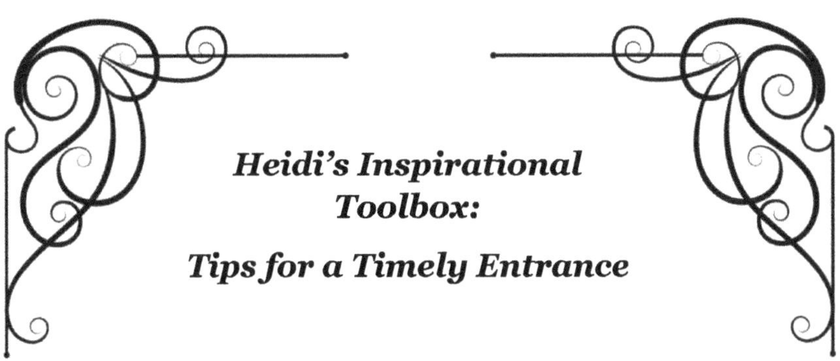

Heidi's Inspirational Toolbox:

Tips for a Timely Entrance

- Plan ahead and give yourself extra time for "fires." Make arriving on time a priority. Get places early so you can relax and feel stress-free.
- Dig deep to uncover the reason behind your chronic tardiness. Ask yourself the hard questions, and seek help, if necessary.
- Make being prompt a priority! Start by being more intentional with your time. Do you get started with a project and have trouble estimating how long it takes? I use the 15-minute rule. Set your timer for 15 minutes, for example, and end your task when the timer goes off, even if you're not done, so you can be on time for your next task.
- Practice boundaries and saying no to projects or people that are taking too much of your time.
- Many of my clients and friends are challenged with saying no. It takes courage to say no to your friends because you soooo want to say yes.

- Here are some of my go-to phrases to help you next time you need to set a boundary:
    - *Thank you so much for thinking of me, but I'm not currently able to commit.*
    - *I would love to, (attend your party, join your nonprofit, meet for lunch);however, I have another commitment (even if that means a quiet bath at home).*
    - *I'm over-booked right now, and the timing doesn't work, but perhaps another time.*
    - *Let me check my calendar and get back to you.*
    - *I don't believe I'm the right person for this project/assignment/client. Let me give you a referral for someone who would be better suited for this situation.*

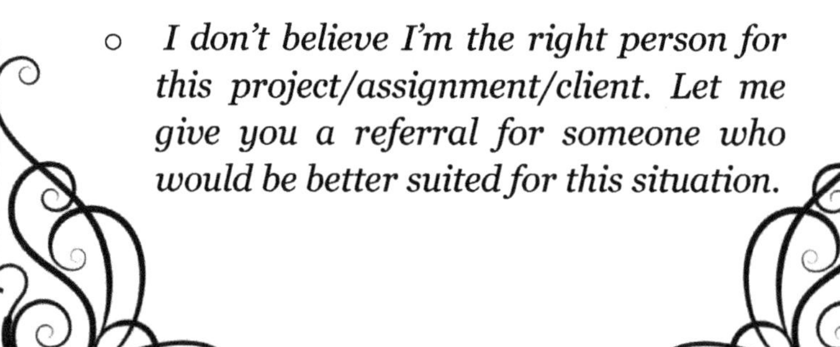

Introducing – The One

Phil

By the time I was 40 years old, I had taken all the self-help seminars on *how to find your guy* that a woman could handle in this lifetime. I worked on myself in therapy, created vision boards, tried speed dating, blind dates, and internet dating, which was just in its beginning stages. I was doing daily affirmations, and basically using all my tools, yet felt I must be blocking something because I still couldn't find my guy. I was ready to give up on love, but a fluttering in my soul remained. My desire was so strong that I found myself praying that my deep longing for a mate would leave my heart. I felt like I was missing out on something. The truth is, I was OK being alone. I traveled extensively by myself. I took myself out to dinner, attended movies by myself, and overall, I was comfortable being with me. I knew I didn't need a man, I just wanted one!

As time went on, I found myself isolating. I got bored and tired of trying so hard to make dating work. I found myself ready to give up on love, but one more venture called. Being in LA, I tried almost everything in the personal-growth area: coaching classes, working out, crystals, prayer and meditation, mindfulness, food cleanses, and the list goes on and on. There was one very LA practice I hadn't tried though: Feng Shui, the Chinese art of placement. Many of my LA friends were fans of this ancient tool and suggested I give it a try. “It will move blocked energy, Heidi. It will help manifest money and your desires." When I researched it even further, it clearly stated you could use Feng Shui to attract and enhance your romantic life. I was sold! And a dear friend of mine had a referral for someone whom she trusted. So, here I go again looking for love and having no idea how Feng Shui would change my life forever!

My Feng Shui consultant—a tiny, dynamic, elderly lady, her long silver hair tied in a bun at her neck—arrived punctually at my apartment for our first consultation. "Ah!" she immediately exclaimed in horror as she entered my apartment. "No wonder you have no man in your life. Too many dames in this place!" She was referring to the many pictures and photographs I randomly collected, mostly of my close female family and friends. Her assessment was correct. "Must go. Must go," she said scurrying about, "immediately." Slight in stature, but mighty in voice; she was strong, authoritative. Next, she pointed to my angel collection, shook her head, and exclaimed, "Ah! All those angels. Too many angels. Must go." She smiled an impish grin, a twinkle in her eye. "No wonder your nights so silent." She giggled, quietly pleased with her little joke.

She mandated I buy pictures of love that I could view daily; a first step, she stressed, is imagining my guy. Despite my reluctance, I asked Courage to help me out and she pushed me to finally purchase *The Singing Butler* (a man dancing on the beach with a woman in a flowing red gown). I also purchased a replica of the famous romantic masterpiece, *The Kiss* (Gustav Klimt). My Feng Shui guru demanded, "Every day you look at those two photos. Imagine the feelings you want to feel. First thing when you wake up in the morning, last thing before you go to bed." Together, we cleared out the clutter in my home: compiling files, tossing out stacks of self-help books.

Then it was time to tackle the closet. That was an area in my life that I just didn't want to look at. There were boxes deep in the corners, and I had no idea what was inside. It was easier to just shut the door and say to myself, *I'll open those boxes on a rainy day.* (It never rains in LA. Ha!)

My enthusiastic consultant—not mincing words—let this be known: "Every box you have in your closet that you don't know the contents of is a metaphor for your life. It represents areas in your life that you have not looked at; that you are avoiding; that you don't want to see. If you want to get unstuck, and see what's holding you back, take out the boxes and go through all the items inside, including old clothing and crumpled papers. Look at your life, Heidi."

Yikes! That was a big ask; however, it was a motivator. Would this really help? I grabbed my sister Courage and decided to give it a try!

Lastly, she said, "You want love and a man? You must make room for him!" She told me to empty a drawer to represent room in my life for him and his things. I was already overwhelmed with limited storage options in my two-bedroom apartment, and it just didn't make logical sense to me. "It must go, it must go," she argued. "You want a man to be comfortable here? Make room for him now for his items. You must get rid of things to bring in the new."

I surrendered to this woman. I'd wake up in the morning and look at (and feel) the feelings that were evoked in this visioning and opened my empty drawer, just waiting.

Sometime later, I flew to New York City to watch the last of my five younger siblings get married. A final blow. I couldn't help but feel devastated. Loser. I could hardly bear attending another wedding where nobody asked me to dance, and I was supposed to act happy? I was happy for the wonderful spouses each of my siblings married; I was just so painfully lonely. And I was giving up hope of ever finding the one for me which made my confidence and charisma plummet.

I stayed in New York after the wedding to visit some college friends. I recall walking along the street to meet my old college roommate Ann, from Ithaca, for sushi. I was busy in my head recalling my brother's wedding, all the jerks I previously dated, and the pain of living my life without a love interest of my own. As I'm having this lively conversation with myself, I noticed a cute, hippy-looking couple, arm in arm, walking along the sidewalk just behind me. As they passed me without stopping, the young man turned and looked back at me, calling out in a weird Hollywood-sounding voice: "You'll get your ring before you die."

And the young couple continued walking. *What?* I thought to myself. *What just happened?* I was stunned. The message directed at me stopped me in my tracks. I shared the incident with Ann at the restaurant. Thank goodness for my pragmatic friend. She just laughed, using her nickname for me, "Whatever you say, Hilda. Whatever you say."

Even though Ann was teasing me, the man's comment gave me hope and peace. I went back to LA with a different attitude. Six months later, in the summer of 2003, I traveled home to Erie. Little did I realize that trip home would change my life forever.

I traveled back to my home in Erie once or twice a year to visit my mom and my sister, and I always returned for my high school reunions. My 25th reunion was soon approaching, and I was still single. But this year, I convinced myself, I was not overly concerned about it. Many of my classmates were divorced. Some were entering into second marriages. I was just excited about being with old friends (or so I kept telling myself). The day prior to the reunion, I went to the cemetery to visit my dad's grave. I found myself kneeling, sobbing, begging for God's help. *I don't care about his looks, age, or occupation,* I prayed. *If there's someone out there for me, God, you find him.*

That evening, I went to a local bar with friends for a pre-reunion gathering. I noticed a handsome guy standing alone at the bar. As he walked across the room, he bumped into me. Blue eyes. Silver hair. Well-built. He didn't look familiar, so I jumped on the opportunity and fired a list of questions at him. My Sisters Confidence, Charisma, and Courage were shaking me, patting my back, shoving me toward him. He shot back with a warm smile. "So, what's with the big personality?"

I was intrigued. Who is this man who really seems to get me and appreciates my charisma? As it turned out, he'd been standing alone at the bar worrying no one would know him. Apparently, he changed dramatically since high school. Our high school class was enormous (more than 700 students). We had never known one another. His name? Philip Frederick Kerner. Nice, I thought. Very nice. For that evening, and the days ahead, we were inseparable. I was only in town for a week, but he took me to the airport for my return to Los Angeles. That night he telephoned. He already booked a flight to LA for the following week. And so, it was to be for the months to follow. Every few weeks, a visit from Phil.

Because Phil and I were both entrepreneurs, our schedules were flexible, and that allowed us to have a romantic long-distance relationship, traveling back and forth from Los Angeles to Erie. In my spare time, I did my research on this guy to make sure he was the real deal. And wow, was I impressed. When I visited his manufacturing business, I was overwhelmed and thrilled to see how productive and successful my future husband was. His building was about 10,000 square feet and hosted 30 employees at the time, working with molding and plastics. *Finally, my knight in shining armor.*

Within a year we were engaged, and I made plans to move back to Erie (something I wasn't willing to do until he proposed). When I did move back, I fell in love with his four sons. The oldest, Matt, really connected with me. He loved his dad and was rooting for this relationship. The youngest was 12 years old at the time. So sweet and funny. I literally visualized *The Brady Bunch*, and for my registry, I even chose more masculine stoneware as I planned on lots of family dinners with the guys.

A journalist heard about our story and contacted me to write an article about us. It was to be featured in a new magazine created by Lifetime TV. They called it "Beauty and the Geek." The tagline on the cover of the magazine said, "I found love at my class reunion!" I finally felt like a star. They interviewed Phil and me, and during his next visit to LA, we had a full-blown photoshoot. I'm talking professional photographer, make-up artist, and hair designer turning my small apartment into a magical creative studio. We took the photos at the beach, and I felt like I had the paparazzi with me. Tourists stopped to take photos of us, I suspect, because they thought we were celebrities. I loved every minute.

What really brought me to tears, though, was publishing day. People I hadn't heard from in years contacted me, inspired by our story. It was exciting! But the best part happened while traveling through the airport. I slowly walked to Hudson Booksellers, giddy and nervous as I approached the magazine stand. Seeing the teaser on the cover, then opening the magazine to our piece and seeing our photos was enough to bring me to tears. I started crying right there. Simultaneously, I wanted to shout and share with the people who were standing next to me, "That's me, that's me!" My new adventure was going perfectly, and my confidence soared. I had my guy, my fame, and was ready to begin my new life.

We planned a wedding in three months, and less than a year after we met, Phil brought me back home to Erie. Finally, as the oldest sibling, it was my turn for marriage. All my cousins and friends from Los Angeles and other parts of the country came in, and we had the most magical night. I even wore red in my wedding dress to symbolize the power of Feng Shui and the photo I had studied daily with the lady in red. My visualizations were reality. I was going to live happily ever after. Finally, I had met the man of my dreams.

Heidi's Inspirational Toolbox:

Tips for Manifesting (Creating) Your Mate

- Make a list—and check it twice—be clear about what you really want in a partner. Then pick one to two deal-breakers. Reference your list often.
- Make room for love, literally. Clear out space in your home or apartment for your soul mate's belongings.
- Use your vision board or photo to visualize your mate.
- Trust the process, and try to surrender your emotions. If your desire is strong, trust that your person is on the way.
- Make the commitment to get out there and date! You can't find the one if you never have a date.
- Practice being the best version of you. You'll be more likely to attract the right person when your head is right.

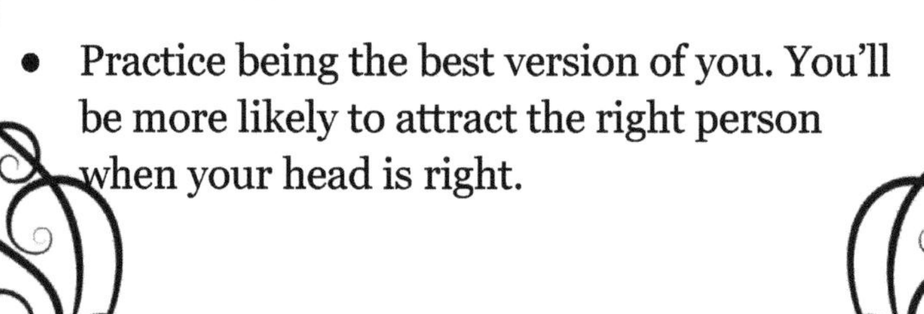

Already Found Your Soulmate? That's not the end of the Journey!

You finally have your forever partner, but now what? Let's talk about how to keep that energy and excitement alive! Creating time alone with one another, remembering what initially brought you together, and how you fell in love in the first place, reinforces your friendship, love, and commitment to your marriage/relationship. Spending time alone enables you to better capture your precious moments of today and yesteryear.

Every Saturday evening Phil and I have date night. Even family and friends know that's our night, and invitations for that evening are usually met with an appreciative, "Thank you but we already have an engagement." And if you remember the Tardy Ts, this also keeps us from overcommitting, rushing, and being late to everything.

We love to get dressed up! No hanging out in sweats on the couch watching TV and ordering take-out for us. When sharing this with other women friends and clients, the usual response is: "Oh, so much effort. I get exhausted even thinking about it." I call it the "magic of dressing up." It provides a transition time that helps elevate one's mood by letting go of our everyday routines.

Take time to set the mood so you can get the most out of your time together. Focus on one another and allow yourselves to just enjoy each other's company. Use the time while dinner is cooking to look each other in the eyes and really connect. Talk with your significant other.

Heidi's Inspirational Toolbox:

Tips for Keeping the Magic Alive

- Continue dating your significant other. Let friends and family know that's your "special night" to avoid hurt feelings.
- Get dressed up. The magic of dressing up helps make your time together special.
- Set the mood. Listen to music. Dance a little. Light some candles.

Act III

Put Your Props in Place

Prop 1 – The Magic Wand

What would you do if you had a magic wand?

I Dream of Jeannie was one of my favorite teenage TV sitcoms ever. The genie, named Jeannie, could blink her eyes to make her wishes come true!

Perhaps you might be more familiar with the fairy godmother in *Cinderella*. The fairy godmother would wave her magic wand, and Cinderella's dreams would come true.

Wouldn't it be wonderful if our goals and dreams could be manifested in the blink of an eye or the wave of a magic wand?

The reason I'm enchanted by a magic wand, and why I often use this as a tool, is because it helps my clients gain clarity with their dreams, passions, and goals. Whenever I physically or metaphorically introduce the magic wand (even with my male clients) I'm first met by a ripple of laughter, followed by silence. A long pause. I watch. I listen. Then I see clients ask themselves, *What if I could actually have what I wanted?*

I find my clients have the most difficulty answering a question that, in fact, is rather a simple one. What do you want next?

There's power in asking that question. I encourage them to play big, dream big, and set goals believing their dreams can become reality. Doing so requires our sister Courage to step in and help us take inspired action. And we can. We can manifest our heart's desires when we gain clarity and focus. It really works!

Kim

When you visit Kim's social media profiles, you see a lovely photo of a 50-year-old real estate agent. Her smile is warm and friendly. Her photo caption reads: "I love my career helping people, making friends, and selling houses." Kim was recently nominated as one of the top realtors in our community. She personifies the profile of the ideal agent. Naturally gregarious, warm, engaging, bright, and articulate—always attractively dressed, whatever the occasion—Kim makes a statement. She has credibility. Her social media posts reflect a motivational emphasis: gratitude for life, playing bigger, and reaching for your dreams.

I met Kim several times through the years, as we seemed to have friends and networking connections in common. However, whenever I ran into her, it was just that, running into her. Whether at the grocery store, networking events, local restaurants, it was always a wave of the hand and a warm greeting with the usual quick small talk, such as, "So, what's new?" and "We must do coffee soon." Finally, we set a date to get to know each other better.

Arriving late at the restaurant, Kim was distracted as she settled into her chair. After relaxing a bit, we comfortably chatted about work, interests, family, and friends. Although never married, Kim has a significant other in her life. She shared how she loved real estate. “I'm good at it. But I really don't want to do it anymore,” she said. “I did advertising. Then I sold jewelry.” She paused, gathering her thoughts. “I think I want to be a health coach. I want to help people.” A deep sigh. “Yet, I can't stay disciplined enough in my own life to work out.”

The restlessness of Kim's spirit was apparent. I further inquired, “Do you ever take time to be quiet. To be still?”

“No,” she said a bit wistfully. “I used to spend time alone. But there's always so much work to be done. I'm always so busy.”

I asked her, “If you had a magic wand, what would your life be like?”

Her response: “I don't know, I don't know. I simply don't know.”

The luncheon was enjoyable, yet I intuitively felt Kim needed something more from me. What could it be? Sometime after our luncheon, Kim joined my women's professional networking group. It was not a surprise that she seldom attended meetings. She was always *too busy*.

Kim's story is familiar to many of us. We say we want something different—something more—but we don’t make time for the *inner journey* to truly discover what that is. It's exciting to know we have a magic wand at our fingertips, but why don't we use it more often? In some cases, we are afraid of getting what we say we want. *Why is that scary?* you might wonder. Because on some level, there is a price to be paid for success. *If I were successful with my dreams, what would others think of me? Would my partner still fit into my picture? Oh, and could I handle all those clients?*

It can be scary to pull back that curtain, to really be seen. You may be tempted to say to yourself, *who am I to live and play bigger? That's not how I was brought up.* To help interrupt this negative self-talk, validate your fear, and get curious. Explore the feeling: where it came from, and how to deal with it. Once you connect those dots, Courage takes over, and Charisma shines. This is what you want. It's OK to claim it!

If you continue to be *too busy* (dancing around the mulberry bush) you'll miss your purpose. We distract and create drama, illness, and chaos all to avoid our true purpose. It doesn't have to be so. Going within to that quiet space, being disciplined enough to stay quiet, doing some journal writing, and reading inspirational quotes are the ingredients that put me on the right track or get me back on track.

The magic wand is a tool to help you focus. It helps you ask yourself simple, yet life-changing questions, keeping you moving in the right direction. The answers will enable you to create priorities and lead a more fulfilling life.

If you could wave a magic wand over your life, business, or career right now, what would you dream? What other questions might you ask? Don't over think it. These questions apply in any situation where one needs greater clarity. Remember, the magic wand is a powerful prop and a daily reminder to keep you inspired and focused so you can play bigger and go higher.

What happened to Kim? She continues to be successful in her career; however, for right now, she's *too busy* to take the time to go within. I believe it will happen one day when she is ready. Are *you* ready?

Heidi's Inspirational Toolbox:

Tips for Manifesting Your Happiest Life

- Ask yourself*: If I had a real magic wand, what would my ideal life* look like?
- Let yourself dream big. Don't limit yourself.
- What's your goal in the next six months? Year? Five years? Write them down.
- Create action steps to help you fulfill the dreams you wrote out.

Prop 2 – The Vision Board

A vision board is a collage of images, pictures, and affirmations illustrating your hopes and dreams. It's a simple poster filled with inspiring images and words that will help manifest (create) your goals. I'm sure you're asking how. A vision board is covered in things that make you feel happy. Images can trigger our impulse to make visions become reality and give us confidence to achieve our dreams. Seeing these images helps us actively think about the goals and dreams we have, and that visualization helps us act on them.

Many of my mentors in the self-development field maintain that you can have many of the things you desire if you are clear on your goals. Have you ever set a goal and not achieved it? Are you someone who makes the same New Year's resolutions, year after year, without ever accomplishing one? You are not alone. It takes time, commitment, and a vivid imagination to achieve the results you want.

I have been creating vision boards for more than 25 years. At the beginning of each year, I ritualistically create a vision board. It sets the stage for the year ahead, it gets me excited, and I can then clearly design my goals to match my intentions. I believe in the power of imagery and visualization. And I have proof of vision boards working many times in my life, as well as for my family, friends, and clients. Many of my vision boards included a well-balanced life. Typical pictures of eating healthy, some exotic travel photos, successful career, friends laughing.

I encourage you to create a vision board if you haven't experienced this tool before. Allow yourself to dream big. Write your goals down.

Ask yourself some questions:

- Big picture: What do I want my next year to look like?
- Personal Life: What would I like in my relationships? More romance? More family time? More connections with friends?
- Career: How is my career or business going? Would I like to make more money? Change jobs? Go back to school?
- Health: Do I need to see the doctor or dentist? Would I like to become more fit? Eat better? Have more energy?
- Home: Is my home comfortable? Is there an area that needs a face lift?
- Fun: Where would I like to go? What brings me joy? Do I need a new creative hobby? Maybe join a Book Club?
- Personal growth: Am I giving attention to the importance of silence and spirituality? Might I consider volunteering, attending lectures, taking a yoga class?

Now it's time to see YOUR dreams depicted on a vision board. Believe you can achieve these images. Here are some of the highlights and results I have experienced because of my vision board:

- Growing my business
- Publishing my first book
- Visiting Greece with Phil—the trip of a lifetime!
- Found our dream house (story to follow in this chapter)
- Dancing and performing

Who inspires you? Put it on your vision board.

* I included a photo of my role model Marie Osmond: Because she inspires me!

If you put images on your board and truly visualize them happening, they will.

What if it doesn't? I truly believe things sometimes take longer because, on some level, we are "blocking it." I know, in retrospect, that was the case for me when I still didn't have "my guy." I never gave up, though.

Every year I cut out the picture of what I wanted my guy to look like and what I imagined we would be like together. I wrote a list of all the attributes I wanted in my guy because I knew the power of writing things down and then visualizing. I went so far as to cut out a picture of my wedding dress and cake. When I finally manifested my man years later, I went back to my early vision board and designed my dress and cake just like I imagined it over 25 years ago!

Jennifer

Jennifer and I met 17 years ago. Yes, she's the same one who is a professional organizer—although she wasn't when I met her—maybe you see where this is going. She was a member of my first professional networking organization. Jennifer, at the time, was in her 40s. Attractive, neatly and professionally dressed, Jennifer exuded a quiet, tentative, almost mousy demeanor. I was impressed that she always wore very stylish high heels. I thought to myself, *there's something more to this gal than meets the eye. I want to get to know her!*

At our networking meetings, each member was encouraged to stand up and do a 30-second elevator pitch. Jennifer stood at the podium before a group of approximately 100 people. Intimidating, I know. With obvious trepidation she looked out at her audience while holding up a single make-up brush (she worked for a company that offered products in the beauty industry). Her voice, hovering above a whisper, said, "I sell make-up brushes," praying, I suspect, that the brushes would just sell themselves. She was very courageous but clearly uncomfortable. To her credit, Jennifer continued with my program.

With time, I got to know Jennifer better. Although a trained esthetician and make-up consultant—affording her a comfort zone at the time—her spirit yearned for more. I came to realize she possessed many skills and talents. I noticed her knack for organization, creativity, cooking, and culinary skills. She had an innate sense of fashion design and color. Household decor came naturally. She graciously shared her abilities with others, giving them suggestions and referrals. There was so much more to her than make-up brushes—not that make-up brushes are a bad thing!

Jennifer lacked confidence in all areas of her life. I perceived her as a *broken bird* (one of my frequent Heidi phrases). When I asked how she felt about herself, she was completely silent. She was unable to reply. Slowly she started sharing. Her parents were divorced. Present family relationships were strained. "I feel I've lost myself. My kids are grown. I feel I'm a caretaker for everyone." She continued, "I don't feel appreciated. When I take a stand on an issue, I feel unsupported. I feel I have been cast into a certain role." She sighed, "I don't know how to audition for another one." She further confided that she longed to help people on their life journeys. Adding, now without hesitation, "I want to make a million dollars." When I mentioned how impressed I felt with her capabilities, she replied, "So, what's the big deal? Doesn't everyone know how to do these same things?" I felt like screaming from the highest mountain: *No, Jennifer. No, they don't!*

One of my tools to help build confidence is affirmations. I encouraged Jennifer to look at herself in the mirror and tell herself: *I am good enough, beautiful, smart, capable, and talented.* Even if some of the words don't feel true or right at this time, do it anyway! I suggested she connect with her sister Confidence and run her through a good workout. She needs to be stretched, strengthened, and massaged.

Jennifer was instructed to create a vision board. Hers clearly defined her goals, values, and what was important to her. Her assignment was to cherish her board. It was to be placed where she could view it daily and to act as if those goals already occurred. Next on Jennifer's agenda: the formation of a business plan.

"Who would hire me?" she inquired.

"Everyone needs a Jennifer," I said.

She soon recognized that the senior citizen population in our community needed a service she felt capable of providing. She felt the call to play bigger.

Today her business is flourishing, helping the elderly downsize and reorganize their lives. Jennifer took the time to clearly define her goals and used her vision board to visualize the outcome! With the help of other women from our empowerment group combined with enormous self-discipline, Jennifer moved away from her comfort zone. She said *yes* to her newly recognized life calling. And yes, she's making money and getting closer to making her financial dreams a reality.

Recently, at my Coffee Club Divas Networking Group's 10th anniversary celebration, I asked Jennifer to share her story with current members about how she built her successful business and gained her confidence. She stood on stage in front of everyone, looking poised in a lovely ensemble, hair styled to perfection with a new shade of red. Her makeup leaving her radiant, and of course, leopard print high heels! She took a pause in front of everybody and breathed in as she owned the room. "This is confidence," she announced with a smile, descending the steps with grace, microphone in hand, she began sashaying among the multitude of tables. In a strong, articulate, enthusiastic voice, she kept repeating the mantra, "I am confidence. Look at me! Always remember to smile, hold your head high, walk with good posture, and own the room." She later added with an impish smile, "I just pretend I'm Heidi!"

The House

Another vision board miracle was how we got our dream house. When Phil and I got married we lived in a very small house that never felt like home. It was older and small but quaint. I was always trying to make the house feel more special. My closet was small, we were too close to the neighbors, and it smelled of old wood. A smell I just couldn't get rid of! We were grateful for our surroundings, yet I was dreaming bigger. This was not my dream house, and I never felt I could really nest there. Where was my house? In so many ways, (even though we were in our 40s at the time) it seemed we were a new young couple just getting started. I was recreating my business in the Erie community, and Phil had a great job, yet buying a new house just didn't seem feasible.

On Sunday afternoons, Phil and I would drive around our beautiful countryside and always enjoyed looking at different neighborhoods. We would often stop to peek into an open house. Phil loved one neighborhood in particular. "This is where I want to live one day," he said. "I love the trees! This feels like a park. This feels like home." I would smile and think *wouldn't that be nice.* However, the homes for sale cost triple what we were paying for our little Cape Cod cottage.

Phil went away for a weekend to a football game, so I was left to putz around on my own. As I was going through the paper, I noticed an open house in the charming neighborhood that Phil loved. I asked my mom, my partner in crime, if she was up for the task of checking it out with me. She was game.

The house didn't disappoint. It was unique; a California ranch (rarer in our area) complete with a dramatic open floor plan. When we walked inside, we were greeted by a beautiful living room. The spacious walls were painted yellow, and we loved the artistic feel to it. Then there was a bonus room ... a sunroom! No matter what the weather, we could enjoy our summer season basically outdoors.

It seemed nobody wanted the house, though. It had been on the market for a while by the time we saw it. *Why?* we asked ourselves. It wasn't a typical home in Erie—certainly not appropriate for the elderly, based on the steps down into the living room—and a bit unconventional for a family with little ones. We felt like it was our house. It was waiting for us. When I told Phil, he was ecstatic. The realtor quickly walked us through; it almost felt devious because the reality was that we were not able to afford the house, much less come up with the down payment or take care of the monthly mortgage and upkeep.

Why were we doing this, wasting this realtor's time? We went home. We looked it up on the internet. We talked about each room. We dreamed about how we would decorate it. We calculated how far we'd be from downtown. We could smell the house. We could taste the house. However, how could we *buy this house*? We knew realistically we were a good year away from being able to even make an offer. Would the house be on the market that long? We continued to drive by the house on our Sunday adventures. Phil would ask, "Do you want to see our house?" Like a little girl, I nodded, "Yes, please." It took everything in me not to pull into the driveway and walk up to the entrance with pride and grace.

Eventually, on one of our Sunday afternoon adventures, we saw movers outside. Someone had bought our house! We were sad, devastated; however, this was to be expected. For some reason, we never gave up hope. Someone else was living in our house, but just for now, we both agreed. A year later, Phil, feeling more confident, decided to contact the realtor about the status of our house. "It's funny you should call," she said. Turns out, a doctor and his wife were renting the house while the husband was in Erie for a medical residency, which is a two-year commitment. However," the realtor continued, "I have heard they want out because they need a bigger place for their growing family." Phil immediately decided we should write them a letter. "Let's find out what's really going on with our house," he said.

Even though it was March, I noticed their Christmas lights were still up: dripping icicles lining the house. I thought to myself, *Wow, that's a unique way to hang lights on the roof. When this is my house, I'm going to do the same thing*. Although inspired and dreaming of my first Christmas in this house, it made the house appear neglected. It was March and the lights were still up? We opened the mailbox and put in our very gentle request that we were looking at this house, and could they give us information about the current owner or their plans to leave the house? It felt a bit like a game, and we were playing detective. The realtor mentioned the owner of the home lived far away. She wasn't sure if it was Arizona? Africa? Or Asia? But far away. The following day we got an email from Asia from the owner of the house. In a simplistic email he said, "Yes, the house if for sale. The renters will be out in a month. Do you want to buy it?" The goosebumps. The excitement. The fear. *Our* house? It's going to happen. But wait. Once again, we were not quite there financially. Almost. So close.

Sometimes I think angels come in different forms. This angel (the owner) certainly didn't seem like an angel with his pragmatic, to-the-point answers. Phil was to set up a phone chat with the owner to discuss finances. As he descended into the basement where his office was, I noticed his tie. "Darling," I asked. "Why the tie?"

"I need to feel the part. I'm a business owner," he said. "I want to negotiate the best deal for this house." He had been talking to my sisters, Confidence and Charisma, and definitely had Courage by his side.

As he was downstairs negotiating, I was upstairs in the bedroom praying. *Lord, I'm asking for a miracle. I don't know how this is going to happen. Yet, I want my house: to enjoy my extended family, to have business networking events, to feel prosperous.* Phil walked into the bedroom after only about 15 minutes, which worried me as it was fast to really dig into a full-blown conversation.

"The house is ours," he said. "He's going to work with us. We move in two months."

"How are we going to keep this up?" I asked.

"We got this far. It's ours, and our business will grow to the extent we need it to fulfill our commitments." We had Confidence on our side!

This May it will be ten years since we happily moved into our house. The power of manifestation unfolds when you begin dreaming big—even when you can't see the big picture. Visualization, images, and a vision board are all tools to help you manifest your dreams; believe that you *can* and *will* achieve your dreams. And again, call on your sisters Confidence, Charisma, and Courage.

Heidi's Inspirational Toolbox:

Tips for Creating Your Vision Board

- Choose images that truly make you feel happy.
- Include a picture of yourself on the board.
- Play. Be creative. Don't overthink the images. Trust the process.
- Place your vision board somewhere you will see it daily. Each morning, stand before it, feel the good feelings and joy the images bring you, and think these are my happy pictures. Then let go, and move on into your day.
- Before you go to bed at night, look at your board to dream about your desire!

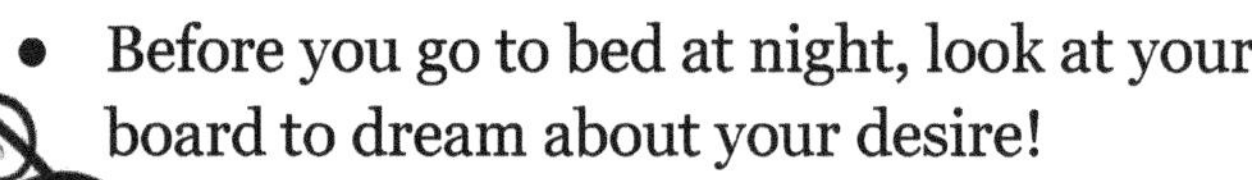

Prop 3 – Movement and Mirrors

The advertisement in the Learning Annex read "The Art of Exotic Dancing for Everyday Women." I blinked a few times, pondering, *What if I? Nooo. Could I? Nooo.* I put the advertisement down but kept it close. After living in LA for 15 years, I thought I'd done it all, but maybe not! I was intrigued. Dare I? Expressive movement, dancing, acting, I loved it all, and as part of my personal growth journey, I decided to take the class. Part of my sudden desire to move my body came from the feeling of losing my sensuality, my feminine energy. I had not been in a relationship for years at this point and felt so disconnected from my body, from myself. For me, the class had less to do with exotic dancing and more to do with transformation, self-confidence, authentic self-expression, freedom, joy, and personal power. The focus was on a powerful expression of oneself.

I bravely asked friend after friend to attend, but no one said *yes*. Not one person. I decided I must still go. On the day of my class, I huddled in my car outside the dance studio. I wore a big hat, dark scarf, and wide sunglasses so as not to be recognized. I watched the women as they approached the entrance. The ages ranged, I estimated, from women in their 20s to, yes, a few in their 70s. They were all shapes and sizes. I glanced into my mirror, *come on, Heidi,* I whispered, *come on.* I felt my sister Courage tapping me on the shoulder. She gave me a "get in there" look, so I stepped out of my car.

What happened in the next three hours changed my life forever. It was, and remains, one of the most powerful experiences of my life. My body felt rejuvenated. I learned that my body, just as it existed that day, was enough. Changing myself wasn't going to change my mind. My mind needed healing first, and this class was a major step.

One exercise was especially intense. Walk up to a life-size mirror slowly, seductively, eyes focused on ourselves. We were encouraged to admire ourselves just as we were: tall, small, fat, skinny, young, old. At the same time, we were to repeat, "I am beautiful. I am beautiful."

I looked at myself, into my eyes, and I felt a sense of serenity. I was beautiful. How could I not love the strong, capable, empowered, faith-filled woman in front of me? And why on earth was I treating her so poorly for so long? My mind-body relationship became clear that day. I realized I needed to move my body from within. I needed to move from the inside out. It was a way to slow down. To rejoice in who I am. To bring so many of the tools together that I accumulated over the years: the mirror work, the affirmations. I felt beautiful. I felt connected to me. I knew I needed to embrace movement for me to feel like my most authentic self. After exotic dancing, I went on to other mindfulness movement classes like belly dancing and African drumming.

As a coach, I recognize the benefit of movement within my professional training groups. I always hire a movement specialist to help support these women in bringing forth their feminine sides. The women usually start by lying on the floor as the instructor helps them center on silence, close their eyes, and feel the music. They are then guided in various creative expressive dance exercises;

sometimes this involves performing emotions such as anger, sadness, and joy (feelings, as women, we sometimes have a hard time expressing). Later, if so inclined, women are asked to do the mirror exercise mentioned above. This is often met with tears, sobbing, defiance. Feelings long repressed are evoked.

Most of the women, however, embrace this new tool. This new awakening. For the first time in their lives, they are learning to dance with their true inner spirit. Witnessing this experience is a beautiful gift to behold.

Heidi's Inspirational Toolbox:

Tips for Movement

- Take the time to look at yourself in the mirror. No judgment. See the beauty. Play some music. Dance.
- Take a belly dancing, African dance, or movement meditation class. Move your body from the inside out.
- Practice mindfulness, and be gentle with your newfound friend. Connect to this beautiful woman, and honor her movements.
- Add some affirmations to say out loud to yourself in the mirror:
- I believe, trust, and have confidence in myself.
    - Today I can handle anything that comes my way.
    - I am beautiful inside and outside.

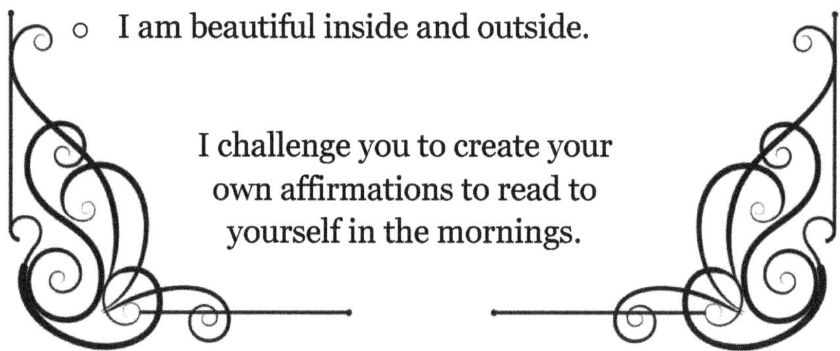

I challenge you to create your own affirmations to read to yourself in the mornings.

Prop 4 – The Mask

Are you wearing a mask? What is it saying to the world?

I believe we all, at one time or another, wear a mask. We often use it as a coping mechanism to protect ourselves. It can be scary and feels very vulnerable to let others see who we truly are. However, at some point in my life, I have found for myself—and the women I coach—that the mask just doesn't serve us anymore.

When COVID-19 hit, I decided it was a good time to wear my masculine hat again. I wanted to fix some areas in my business, write this book, and get back on track. So I began sitting at my desk all day, learning tech to be on Zoom, and reaching out to old contacts to create a global network. Those are the good aspects. I also stopped eating right and stopped exercising. Talk about masks: from the neck up, I looked the part! What was my mask saying to the world? It certainly wasn't showing my authentic self.

There are times in our lives when wearing a mask is important. Typically, the mask is a coping mechanism used to protect ourselves from emotional harm or vulnerability. It can be scary for others to see the real us. It's easy to hide behind a mask when we're unsure of our power, but at some point, the mask no longer serves a purpose. It becomes a stumbling block, or a crutch, and it keeps us stuck. Perhaps the worst part is that we know it is detrimental for us, yet we continue to use it to cope with our insecurities. Inherently, we know there are other ways to cope, but we are unsure how to do it. Taking off our masks and allowing ourselves to be vulnerable is the path to power. This is where the true heart connection lives.

As a seminar leader in women's empowerment groups, I use an intense exercise to help women understand the power of the mask. I ask attendees to literally put on a mask and then have them share how the mask has benefited them. We then caringly discuss the removal of the mask. We create goals for the year ahead, including how to live without the masks. They walk into the seminar room, and on their chair is a simple masquerade mask (just covering their eyes). It's fascinating to me that when I ask the women, "What mask are you wearing? What are you hiding from the world?" the answers come spontaneously. These women were very aware of the masks they are wearing and why they were wearing them. The challenge, however, is not just to name the mask but to take it off.

Emma

At 37 years old, Emma, was one of the youngest to join my empowerment group. She enhanced her naturally exotic look with dramatic makeup and style. Be it early in the morning, or late in the evening, Emma was dressed up from head to toe. However, when I would look at Emma, I felt I couldn't see her. I couldn't find her. I couldn't connect with her. Why? She always had a lot of what I call *bells and whistles* in how she presented herself. Don't get me wrong,

Emma is beautiful and stylish, yet between the considerable makeup, false eyelashes, purple hair, curious hat, nose rings, funky glasses, ornate key chains hanging from her belt, mismatched pants, blouse, and jacket, she was completely swallowed up! I often thought, "Where are you, dear girl? Who are you?" There were so many distractions. I truly wanted to find the real Emma. I wanted to make that deeper connection.

One day, I cautiously asked if she'd consider coming to a gathering without her theatrical garb (which we clearly discussed, and she admitted to it being a mask she was wearing). "Oh no, Heidi," she replied defiantly. "Nobody sees me without my make-up. I'm ugly. You have no idea what it takes me every day to create this look." She giggled. "Hours and hours." I knew this caused Emma anxiety. Yet, how I longed for a breakthrough. I know Emma trusted me. She knew my coaching was coming from love. Emma was also my social media assistant, and she truly is an artist and very creative in her business.

When the group gathered next, Emma (bless her courage) arrived making a dramatic entrance. Wearing large Audrey Hepburn sunglasses to hide the fact that she wasn't wearing makeup, she waltzed into the room sporting a T-shirt and sweatpants, mimicking me and waving a magazine where I had been on the front page. She used it to cover her face.

Emma was met with applause and warm, genuine affirmation of her natural beauty. At least for a moment, she took off her mask. And what happened that day? We had a special speaker who discussed opportunities for writing blogs. She was so impressed with Emma that she hired her on the spot. As a result of Emma being seen through her writing, she was nominated for Woman of the Year (Women Making History) and an award called Erie's 40, honoring this younger generation and the difference they are making.

Even though Emma immediately went back to wearing her mask after this powerful meeting, I believe her experience of *letting go* that day changed her. Emma grew from doing something outside of her comfort zone through the support of this group—and without it, she would have never had this amazing opportunity. Although this lovely, bright, and vibrant young woman isn't ready to ditch the mask entirely, her social media business is growing, and her charisma is intact. She acknowledges the day she felt safe taking off her mask and the acceptance she received from others in her life. She admits the *struggle is still real* and that she continues to search for the true Emma. And that's OK!

Meghan

I have a similar story about another woman in my empowerment group named Meghan, referred to by all who are privileged to know her as Magnetic Meghan. Warm, gregarious, highly intelligent, creative, motivated, Meghan is like a living doll in every sense of the term. She is pretty, meticulously groomed, lots of glamour and glitter, and always has a smile on her face. You can't help but think, *Is she for real? To hug and hold? Or better still, to place on a living room shelf of cherished items for others to admire?* When I asked, with trepidation, if she would attend a gathering without her makeup and fancy outfits, she replied without hesitation, "No, Heidi. I will not. I'm not comfortable with that assignment." As a long-time cherished networking group member, I reminded her that the purpose of our group was to better enable us to move out of our comfort zone and trust the process.

Meghan arrived at the following meeting without the jewels and without the makeup. Always serene, she was obviously very angry at me. She expressed the pain she experienced with this assignment and considered leaving the group. But with all the anguish she endured, she did it! Meghan received such genuine love and admiration from the women emphasizing how they each love her dearly and cherish her for who she is, not for a role she is trying to play. They wanted Meghan to be her authentic self so her natural charisma could shine through. As we moved on with other topics in the group, I noticed Meghan slowly replacing her jewelry as well as her lipstick. She gave us a small glimpse of her authentic self. And that's OK!

Although Meghan returned to the comfort of her mask, a transformation occurred that day. She took my advice; she trusted the process; she trusted the women in the group; and she allowed them to really see her; and ... it was good. She learned that they loved her for her authentic self, her caring heart, her nurturing spirit, and ... it was good. This was a painful exercise for Meghan, but she chose to grow from it.

And guess what? At age 72, Meghan just completed her first published book, which has become a top rated read on Amazon! Her personal motto that she shares with all women who seem stuck: "Feel the fear. Do it anyway."

We often wear masks to hide our true selves. We are afraid that if people see the real us, we won't be accepted. It takes courage to take off the mask. To allow others to see the real you. To allow charisma to take over and explore what that feels like. There is no harm in asking why we present ourselves to the world in the way we do; in fact, it's critical we do some radical self-examination. Too often, we allow our mask to show instead of our charisma, which isn't the best groundwork for self-improvement. Removing the mask (even if it's just from time to time or for a few hours) is key to interacting with our vulnerability. And vulnerability leads the heart to love. Isn't that what it's all about anyway?

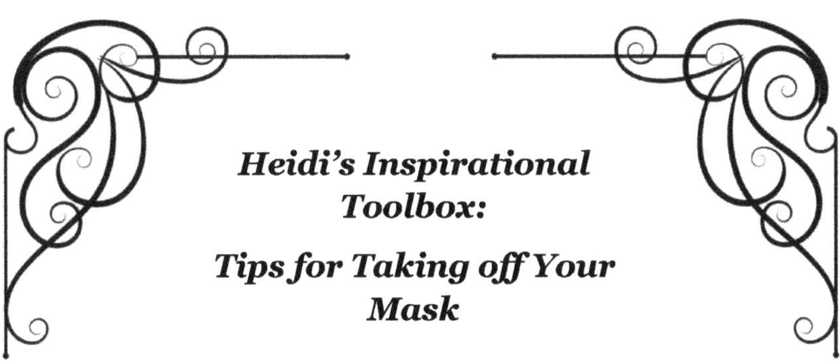

Heidi's Inspirational Toolbox:

Tips for Taking off Your Mask

- What mask you are wearing? Perfection? Anxiety? Busy disease, distraction, self-doubt, or the funny girl? How is it serving you? What would it be like for you to take it off?
- Journal around your feelings. Are you ready to let the fear around your old self go?
- Try going somewhere without the mask you usually wear, and see how it feels.
- Think about how you would act, talk, walk if you weren't wearing a mask?

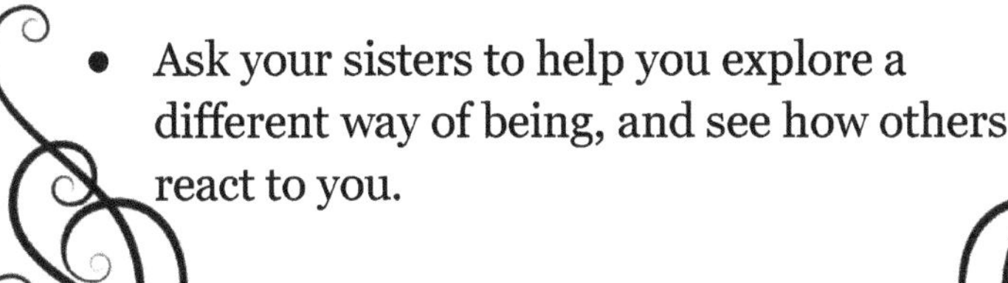

- Ask your sisters to help you explore a different way of being, and see how others react to you.

Act IV

Stepping into the Spotlight!

Scene 1 – Coming Back Home

My time in LA left me, I believed, with all the tools I'd need professionally and personally to succeed. Little did I know I'd need to lean on them so much in the coming years. It was show time, and I thought I was prepared. I thought I was ready. I had my sisters by my side: Confidence, Charisma, and Courage. I just had the wedding of a lifetime—the most beautiful wedding I could have dreamed of. I was the star of my life and loved every moment of it. *So, what's next?* I asked myself. I was stepping into the unknown, but literally coming back home to Erie. A strange, but exciting juxtaposition. Here we go—lights, camera, action!

At the time, Phil was living in a little cottage in the woods meant for a bachelor, and I was excited to move in, be surrounded by the woods, spark a fire every night, and get away from the noise of my LA lifestyle. But the minute we got married, everything changed. China was taking over manufacturing during this time, and Phil's business was going down fast. Within the first two months of getting married, he started selling his equipment, was laying people off, and put the building up for sale. *OK, for better or worse,* I thought. *We will figure it out.*

Then, right after we were married, one of Phil's sons moved in with us. At first, I was excited to be a stepmom, but within a couple of weeks, it became clear that there were some serious boundary and addiction issues at play. *Why was this happening to me?* I waited until my 40s to find a family, and this is what years of quiet discernment and patience afforded me? It was selfish, but I couldn't help but feel like I was cheated out of a new romantic life with my husband. How could my world come crashing down so quickly?

We would try to go out on date nights even though Phil was now working a second shift. How did I end up having such lonely nights, often eating dinner alone? Things were just not working out as I planned. One Saturday, we did manage to go out for an evening of dinner, wine, and conversation. Phil was tired, which was typical after a hard work week, but he insisted we go out and said he'd feel better once we were out. We really cherished our date nights, which is why I was struck when we were seated at our table and his coloring looked a little off to me. I asked if he was OK. "I'm just a little tired still," he said. I hesitated for a moment but asked, "Do you want to leave?"

"Yes," he said. I was shocked by his answer because a glass of wine usually cures all aliments. When we stood up to go pay the bill, I saw sweat on his face. Looking at him, I knew something was seriously wrong. "Do I need to take you to the hospital?" I asked. He immediately said *yes*. I was terrified but tried not to show it. Sister Courage held my hand. I drove him right to the ER (thankfully we were only a few minutes away). The minute we walked in, they knew he was having a heart attack. I stayed with him that night. The next day he underwent surgery to put stents in. I prayed, *Please God, I've waited for this man my whole life. Please don't take him away from me this early in our marriage.*

Thank goodness we were already out and minutes away from the hospital that night. The surgeon said that if he stayed at home and went to sleep, he wouldn't have made it.

Thank God he made it and for the healing that came. Were my prayers being answered after all? Just in the most unusual way?

We carried on with life as normally as possible. Going to the boys' games was a ritual I enjoyed. They were athletes, and it was common for us to attend one to two sporting activities a week. I quickly noticed, however, that whenever I walked into a sporting event, the women stopped, looked me up and down, and turned away without acknowledgment. People did not welcome me.

I was so confused. Did I do something wrong? Why was I always accepted in LA but not here? Did I make a mistake moving here? Talk about not fitting in; I never felt so hurt and alone. I thought I conquered my shame and bullying issues in the past. I walked into these events with my head high, but it was exhausting to believe I was being gossiped about and feel unaccepted.

In the meantime, I wasn't quite ready to move into business mode again. After marriage, I wasn't planning to work again except with a few chosen clients. However, with the changes happening in Phil's business, it became a necessity, and I realized I needed to go back to my sisters Confidence, Charisma, and Courage to rebuild the business of my dreams. Because Phil previously attended many of my networking events in LA, we decided to reinvent ourselves and start our first networking group together in Erie.

After 20 years in LA, and having a successful coaching business, I was excited to share my experience with Erie's business community. Professional networking, I soon realized, was relatively limited locally. We decided to use the model I followed in Los Angeles: going door-to-door with our flyers inviting businesses to attend our first meeting. We were met with a this-will-never-work attitude, which shocked me but did not deter me.

I remember walking into a women-owned business, sharing my excitement about our new group. In front of her customers she said, “We don't need this group. It's a manufacturing town. You are wasting your time.”

I felt my anger build. In Los Angeles, I was always met with so much support. Everyone was so encouraging. I was out of my comfort zone and frankly confused. I found myself giving her a little pushback. “How can you say that? This is a woman-owned business. Why would you not support someone like me who’s from this town and just moved back?”

She just looked at me, disgusted, and after close to 17 years back in Erie, I have never returned to her shop. Some people just aren’t going to get it, and all I can do is provide opportunities to grow. I can’t make people take them. This was my first wakeup call: I was no longer in Los Angeles and quite frankly didn't understand *where* I was!

After another day of dropping off flyers to local businesses, Phil and I were ready for a break. Happy hour sounded good to us. We stopped by a beautiful local bar and restaurant, got comfy on the couches, and processed our day. I was distracted by a group of very attractive women sitting at a table enjoying their cocktails. There must have been about ten women. I watched them. I was so intrigued by how they presented themselves in their dress. They looked like my kind of gals! I arrived in Erie a few months prior and wasn't used to seeing women dressed up. The sharp haircuts, tailored suits, fishnet stockings? I was in heaven. I wanted to be their friend. I didn't have any new friends in Erie and was hungry for female companionship.

With enthusiasm, I said to Phil, "I'm going to walk over to that group of gals, say *hello*, and invite them to the meetings. Don't they look fun? Don't they look LA fresh?"

I was surprised by Phil's hesitation. "Are you sure you want to approach them? Why don't we just wait and relax. You don't want to bother them."

"Oh please," I said. "This is right up my alley. I got this!"

As I approached the table, I put my sisters Confidence and Charisma on my shoulders. I was the networking queen in Los Angeles. I learned how to approach tables of folks I didn't know. I put my smile on and basically shimmied up to the table. The first step in charisma (aside from an approachable smile), is to compliment!

"Hello gals!" I said, "Wow you all look amazing! I just moved to Erie from out of town, and I wanted to introduce myself."

Dead silence. The women looked at each other and then at me like I literally had five heads.

Finally, one woman spoke up. "Hi, I'm Charlotte."

My networking chops taught me that sometimes folks get caught off guard, so as my acting teacher would remind me, *Be present Heidi. Play off their energy Heidi. Go in for another chat.*

"I'm excited to start a networking group here in town. This is what I did in Los Angeles. I know they have a couple of other groups in town, yet mine would be a little different. I'm looking to have meetings where we do self-introductions, keep each other accountable with our goals, and bring in motivational speakers to inspire us personally and professionally."

Again. Nothing. Finally, another woman said, "This is a blue-collar town. We are attorneys. I don't even know who I'd give your flyer to. Certainly not right for us."

My courage was gone. The old feelings of shame came back. I felt silly. It reminded me of not getting picked to play on the team during my grade school gym classes. I felt they were the popular girls and almost like they were bullying me. I walked back to Phil deflated.

"How did that go?" he asked.

"Not so well," I said in a meek depleted voice.

"I told you so, darling." He squeezed my hand in sympathy. "Welcome to Erie. You are no longer in LA. Let's get another glass of wine." That sounded good to me!

The next step was for Phil and me to drive to the ballroom where we visualized having 100 business owners attend our first meeting. We knew we were taking a risk. We looked at the empty space, prayed quickly, and affirmed we could do this. We pushed on. Despite a rough start, we believed there was room for us here. Within five weeks of deciding to create a networking group, we finally held our first meeting ... and applause, 100 people attended! Business people in the community and local entrepreneurs got word there was something a little different going on, and they were curious to check it out!

I was in my glory performing on stage each month, sharing my nuggets of business tools and techniques sprinkled with inspiration and motivation. I loved working with Phil on our team venture. We were getting recognition and a decent paycheck, and we knew we were making a difference. Our members were getting clients and learning how to network.

Always interested in taking our clients to the next level, we hired a focus group for feedback. We anticipated eventually opening more local chapters and perhaps chapters elsewhere. What did the members want more of? How could we improve our business model? How could we enroll more clients?

It's always a bit daunting knowing your members will be *talking behind your back*. However, it's a great way to get honest feedback with the thought they will be more comfortable sharing information with an outsider. Laughingly, Phil and I conjured up what they might come up with. We knew they didn't like the early morning time. They complained about the paper name tags. And I knew they wanted more variety in their meal choices. Other than that, we didn't know what else they might want.

When it was time to discuss the results with our consultant, we chose an Italian restaurant that's been around since the late 1930s. Big leather booths. Gaudy pictures on the wall. Small vases of red, plastic flowers and baby's breath over white-paper-covered tables. It looked like a *Goodfellas* set (and still does). Erie is old school, and I love the town's old-fashioned values.

The organizer began by validating our work.

"You're doing a great job. I believe the community needs the skills you are both bringing to the table." She paused, and said, "But I'm confused. I don't understand the feedback. It really makes no sense to me." Again, she paused. Then continued, "The recommendation is that Phil should stay, and Heidi should go."

"What do you mean?" Both Phil and I exclaimed looking confusingly at each other.

"Well, it seems the feedback says Heidi is 'too much.' They don't want to play bigger. They don't want to learn public speaking and networking skills," she said. "They like the group, but Heidi is just 'too much.' Too much personality. Too much energy. Over the top. We can't relate. We don't like her. We like Phil."

Under the table I pinched myself. Hard. I was trying to hold back the tears that were on the surface. I wanted to be professional. To act like it didn't bother me. To take the criticism accordingly. What was frustrating, however, was the feedback was not specific. There were no action steps for me to take. My confidence again shattered; I was taking this personally. *What's wrong with me?* I thought. As I continued to pinch my hand, which was turning red and hurting, I felt a cold sore coming on. Just like that. My body was so quick to react to this news that it took away my confidence, my charisma, and my courage. It shattered my spirit.

The world around me collapsed. I held it together until we got in the car, where I had a massive meltdown. Poor Phil truly didn't know what to do with me. The pain was so great. The wound so deep. They win.

I vowed to never do another speaking engagement for our group. And I didn't. For nearly a year Phil took over as the group leader, teaching new networking tools, presentation skills, and communication techniques. I was behind the curtain, coaching him at home each month on how to present our topics. The group loved him. He continued to grow as a strong, confident public speaker. I still attended each event with him, sitting in the front row, cheering him on. I was genuinely happy for him, but I still pondered why I affected the group so strongly. More so, I was confused.

In the interim, I wallowed in my despair and anger, trying to comprehend where I failed. I hired a coach. I went into therapy. With professional encouragement I dug deeply into the psychological components possibly involved: Could it be they believe I think something of myself that I do not? Was I projecting something that is not my authentic self? There can be a fine line between perception and reality. In retrospect, when I was traveling as a speaker, and when I told a Midwestern audience I was from LA, I sensed a subtle shift of mood in the auditorium. Or had I imagined it? A communication breakdown?

I studied. I did more research. My dad was a blue-collar guy. Both grandfathers were blue-collar guys. My husband is a blue-collar guy. What I failed to consider was that we attracted a blue-collar population into our group. In time, with support and intense personal growth, I slowly, very slowly, healed.

It finally dawned on me that in Los Angeles, most folks are transient, not from the city. They are welcoming of strangers because they are one. Plus, the sunshine really does add an extra element of happiness. I learned that it's OK that the population here wasn't as open to learning. However, I pondered how I could meet them in the middle. How can I be me, teach what I love, and be more aware of my audience?

It's then that I learned to not take it personally. It truly wasn't about me. I was different. I represented big dreams. They were uncomfortable with that. It was unfamiliar. As a professional speaker with a great deal of experience, I must continue to learn ... always.

As a seminar leader and with all the subjects I have been teaching over the years, there is a struggle that we all share: taking things personally. Who knew? I thought it was just me. At the beginning of a seminar, I often place Q-Tips on chairs (and watch participants recoil in disgust). The Q-Tip represents *Quit Taking It Personally.* I begin, "How many of you have a hard time letting go when someone has done or said something to you that puts you in a state of self-doubt?" or "How many of you have experienced hurt feelings? Felt frustrated?" Ninety percent of my audience raises their hands. I'm always impressed with their honesty. I share with them that I, too, have been hurt. Frustrated. I used to take everything personally. It was often crippling and kept me stuck in all areas of my life.

So, how can we stop doing this to ourselves? *The Four Agreements*[1], a popular book by Don Miguel Ruiz, became my constant companion. The second agreement is focused on not taking everything personally. This was a real head-turner. When people confront—attack—you, directly or indirectly, it has nothing to do with you. It is a projection of

---

[1] Don Miguel Ruiz, *The Four Agreements* (Amber-Allen Publishing, 1997)

their own life and innermost thoughts. Other people's reactions are a combination of their own backgrounds, shattered dreams, inability to play bigger, and their own fears. It has nothing to do with you. This can be hard for us to realize because most of us live at the center of our own universe; we spend a lot more time thinking about our thoughts and actions than anyone else does.

Try not to take it personally. What people say about you reflects on them, not you. With professional support—and ongoing, loving input from my LA circle of friends—I learned a new way of presenting myself. When I finally decided it was time for me to get back up on stage at our networking group a year later, I simply and more quietly introduced myself saying: "My name is Heidi Parr Kerner, and I am from Erie, Pennsylvania." Our business was successfully sold a year later to a straight-shooter Erie gal who was perfect for the job. Phil returned to his manufacturing career. I went online, creating a worldwide client base through the internet and webinars. Networking was how I built my business and lifelong relationships in LA. I missed the camaraderie and connections that face-to-face networking bring.

One Saturday morning, four years after we sold our business, the early autumn air was crisp, clear; I awoke, lingering in bed. A little voice within whispered, *Heidi, it's time. It's your time. Let your voice be heard.* Like a mantra, it kept repeating. Mysterious, I thought. My courage was brewing.

I decided to dip my toes in one more time. I asked on Facebook if there were any women entrepreneurs who might be interested in getting marketing support, presentation skills training, and networking tips, and if so, would they like to meet for coffee to build business relationships? Thus, the Coffee Club Divas was born, a networking organization for women in my newly reclaimed home of Erie. At my first coffee meeting, 20 women showed up. I asked if they wanted to meet again, and they did. The second month, 25 women attended. Today, we have over 150 members and celebrated our tenth anniversary this year.

It took a lot of courage to recreate myself. To say *yes* to something uncomfortable. However, I believe if I stayed in the *hurt*, or stuck, I would not have been able to help the hundreds of women who have come my way through my Coffee Club Divas network.

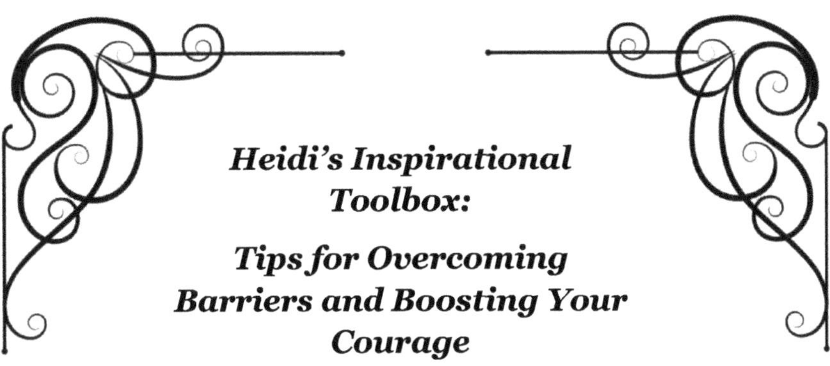

Heidi's Inspirational Toolbox:

Tips for Overcoming Barriers and Boosting Your Courage

- Q-TIP: Quit Taking It Personally
- First understand your audience, or the personality of the person you are connecting to. How can you meet them where they are?
- Feel the fear, and do it anyway. Fear is a natural part of courage. It's OK to feel the fear, but try to move past it. What are you being called to do?
- People need your gifts! You must have the courage to override your pain and think bigger.

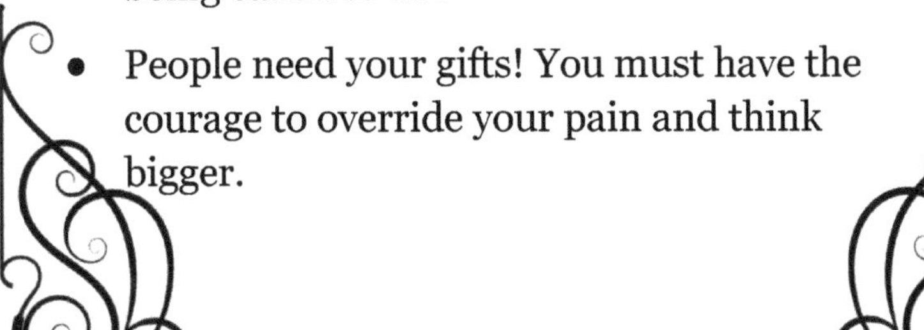

Scene 2 – Life and Loss

Loss. It's not something we usually associate with success and living a joyful life that we love. But the truth is that all of us have to deal with it. Sometimes multiple times in our lives. Usually when we least expect it.

I wanted to share about my experience with loss to help you navigate loss when you bump into it. It's not pretty, but learning how to gather support from your three sisters, Courage, Confidence, and Charisma means that when loss is center stage, you know how to navigate it better than if you didn't have those sisters on your side.

I've been in both a supporting and a leading role in several instances of loss in my life, and I'm thankful every day for how I've been able to build myself into the woman I am today, so I can better deal with it.

I was a toddler when my parents brought my baby brother home from the hospital. His tiny presence only lasted three weeks. On a gentle April day, with no warning of the impending loss to come, my little brother suddenly died.

A "subdural hematoma," the doctors said. There was "nothing you could have done," he told my parents.

In time, five more children came to join our family, but whenever someone asked my mother how many children she had, she would always reply, "We have seven children, but one is already home in heaven."

And so, she does to this day.

Jimmy, my brother who passed away as a baby, is our family saint. His stay was but a whisper in time; yet his presence will last forever.

As the years passed and more little ones joined our family, our already limited living quarters grew even smaller, so the newest Parr baby and I would often share a room together. Folding diapers, fetching bottles, picking up toys, entertaining the little ones ... I was proud to be proclaimed as my mother's helper. I recall my mother asking me as the toddlers happily babbled in their baby talk, "Whatever are they saying, Heidi? What does all that gibberish mean?" I always knew.

Protective as I was, as the children grew older, I teased my little brothers and sisters mercilessly. I told them that the piano bench in our living room, covered with a bright floral needlepoint design against a black background, was, in fact, their brother Jimmy's coffin. They would run and scream in terror. Chaos. Absolute chaos.

My mother later told me that I attended Jimmy's funeral service and burial on that warm spring morning, but did I? I don't remember. Deep in my subconscious, did I connect his shiny white coffin covered with jonquils and tulips with the bright piano bench tapestry lovingly stitched by my Aunt Rose? Interesting. Can a toddler's tiny brain retain an image that emerges later in childhood? This was my first experience with death: so small, yet still so impactful. Of course, it wouldn't be my last.

I was obviously too young to fully remember Jimmy passing. So, my first true experience of death was of my father's. My dad died at age 64 of complications due to

Parkinson's disease. He was a pillar in the community and held a prestigious title at the bank. To watch this strong six-foot-four man shrivel away was heartbreaking.

Toward the end, a hospital bed was placed in my parent's bedroom. Nurses came and went. My father, although different looking now (so thin and frail) also possessed a different energy. Some of our best talks were during these times. In the past, our conversations were mostly about my work and business. Now he wanted to hear about me, my relationships, and what makes me happy. I loved that part of my father but had missed it during my growing up years.

During his illness, I was living in Los Angeles, and I would fly home on a regular basis to visit. Toward the last six months of his life, when hospice came in, we were told several times, "This is it," and all my siblings who lived around the world (my brother was living in China) would fly home for our last goodbyes. Ironically, we learned later that he would magically come back to life seeing all the kids and the energy we brought him. He was in a hospital bed, but at least he was home.

His humor remained intact until the end. Despite his Catholic upbringing, his sense of humor was naughty at times. He loved limericks, especially the off-color ones! We shared our limericks, sang our favorite songs, and left Erie once again with heavy hearts, thinking each time that this was probably the last time we would see him. And then one day, it was.

The funeral was personal. My father loved hats. Silly hats. Whenever he and my mom hosted parties, they wore hats. I guess this is where I got some of my costume and play inspiration. Over the years we collected lots of hats. Boxes of them. When we went to the cemetery for the burial, each attendee grabbed a hat to wear. I know my father would have loved this. Lots of laughter through the tears as you looked around and saw so many people wearing these silly hats. We then took off our hats at the cemetery and left them so my dad would be buried with them.

Grieving my dad is a long process, even with Courage by my side. His passing was sad. I mourned my loss. However, it was expected—not easy—but expected. What I was not ready for was the next loss that would enter our lives and change how I looked at death forever.

At the time of our marriage, Phil had four sons, aged 12, 14, 17, and 21. Handsome, bright, articulate, fun, funny. Strong athletes. Affectionate. The boys were close. I loved seeing how they comfortably hugged and interacted with their dad and with one another. I really did have a vision of *The Brady Bunch* in my head, but our blended family fantasy did not last long. The family dynamics shifted. Slowly. At first imperceptibly, then ruthlessly. A cruel, relentless intruder entered our home. His name? Drugs. Our family life shattered.

All four boys. All at different stages in their addiction. Approximately at the same time. Stealing. Cars disappearing. Late-night phone calls for pick-up. It was a vicious cycle. We just didn't know how to make it stop. Calls from the police station, jail, rehabilitation centers—a rinse and repeat cycle that went on for years. My work as a therapist prepared me for the patterns, manipulations, and co-dependency I saw evolve in my new family. For greater support, I entered a 12-step program for friends and family of addicts to help better understand my new reality. There were a lot of sleepless nights and prayers. We spent a lot of time arguing about what was best for the boys. It was taking a toll on our relationship. I couldn't believe I finally married at the ripe old age of 44, and even with all the personal growth work I did, I never anticipated this coming. How didn't I see the signs? Did I rush into this too quickly?

Then came the public shame and embarrassment. There was no hiding from it. We found out that one of my stepsons embezzled a significant amount of money from a company he worked for—in the name of drugs—and was consequently arrested. We also found out the local paper was planning to print the story. Phil and I aggressively reached out to that paper with the help of our many networking contacts. We pleaded and negotiated for them to drop the article, but it was done. We braced ourselves for the worst, as it still loomed ahead.

I called my mom to explain what happened. I was so sad and scared. My parents worked hard in this community, and their name meant something; my father's legacy was important to me. My husband's name was also a legacy in this town. His family name was synonymous with a successful manufacturing business for over 100 years. How could we brace ourselves for this fall? I felt so hopeless and alone. Phil struggled with his own pain, watching one of his children put himself in this position. He couldn't be there for me, and I didn't know what to do with my deep feelings. Humiliation. Anger. Regret. Sadness. Shame. I've dealt with shame before but never *public* shame. I truly didn't know if I would survive.

Then the article was released. Why did they have to print his photo, making the article stand out even more? I kept bargaining in my head, *maybe nobody will notice?*

Nobody really reads the paper anymore. Do they? Not only was there a photo, but they put our mailing address, too, even though he wasn't even living with us at the time. That same afternoon, a company I worked with emailed me politely, and vaguely, stating they no longer needed my services. Coincidence? I think not. I was shocked—just earlier that week, they confirmed continuing work with me, and worst yet, there was still a $5,000 outstanding invoice with them. I expected my stepson's actions to affect my emotional health, but my paycheck? I couldn't believe it.

I had an in-person speaking engagement the following week and was terrified of going. Who knew what would happen? Were they talking about me behind my back? Does it indicate what bad parents we are? Was it my fault? The anxiety I felt was crippling, but I called on my sister, Courage, and showed up anyway.

One woman approached me and asked, "Are you Heidi ... related to Phil?" My heart stopped. I almost blacked out.

I meekly said, "Yes?"

"Oh, I know him from the bowling days," she said. I was filled with relief.

My anxiety, loneliness, and humiliation were deep. These feelings lasted for months. *Why did I move back here? Why did I get married to someone with kids?* I felt so forgotten by God.

I don't know if it was a dream or real, but I believe I was visited by the Angel of Death. There were times in my past where my depression was so consuming that I didn't want to go on. I fought it in therapy and through God's grace.

This time, I made the decision I wasn't going to let this break me. I dearly loved my husband, my friends, my networking community, and these boys!

A cutesy family sign reading "Hope Joy Happiness" hung in our kitchen. I contemplated taking it down but left it hanging. Hope. There was always hope. We understood that the boys were in pain. We tried to help them: love, therapy, support, compassion, but ultimately, we needed to practice tough love and to stop enabling them. We knew that with addiction there were consequences. Jail. Rehab. Death. We just didn't realize we'd experience all three.

I visited a prison once as a child during a school tour designed to terrify kids to stay out of jail (you could still do that in the '60s), and yes, it was scary and sad. That was the only time I'd ever seen a jail on my own. I never knew anyone who had been incarcerated before.

I remember the first, and only time, I went to visit one of my stepsons in jail. I wondered if it would be like on a TV episode. Would there really be a phone behind the Plexiglas partition? Would he be wearing an orange suit? Would I cry? Would I be encouraging? Would he be handcuffed? These were my thoughts as we traveled to the jail during visiting hours that Sunday afternoon. There was a resounding *yes* to all the questions above. It looked and felt just like TV. He wore an orange jumpsuit. We teased and laughed a bit as we put our hands together on the glass wall. I was teary. I was encouraging. I imagined what jail would look like, but I didn't imagine the depth of pain and sickness I felt in the waiting room.

When I first walked into the visiting area, I sensed a heaviness in the air. I felt like I couldn't breathe. Sadness permeated the stale room. I wasn't expecting so many children to be there. Time seemed to slow down. I watched the clock. I watched as adults were trying to keep their children under control. I watched the security guard standing so stoically, calling each family in one by one. I ached for everyone but especially the children. Why does the disease of addiction create so much pain in people's lives? I wanted to vomit. Phil was reading the paper silently as I watched the children wait. I needed fresh air. "I'll be right back," I said. I needed to get out. I needed to remember and feel there was life outside this cave.

Outside, I was reminded of my broken dreams. I was once so excited to welcome these boys into my life, to have the happy family I always imagined. How can I ever fulfill my bigger life purpose when I'm chained to this stressful life I am now living? I felt little courage stepping back into the waiting area; that's the thing though, sometimes taking that extra step gives you the courage to keep walking. Just showing up really is the solution to most of our problems.

A few weeks later, on a peaceful Saturday evening, January 11, 2014, Phil, and I were taking down the Christmas tree. The holidays were over, and we we're anticipating a quiet, relaxing evening. The telephone rang a little after 9 p.m. Phil answered, "OK, uhuh. OK." Pause. "What's the address?" he asked. I wasn't overly concerned. Late-night phone calls were not unusual. To be honest, I felt annoyed. It was the holidays; we'd almost made it through without incident. *What now?* I thought. Phil put down the phone. Expressionless, he looked at me and said, "Matt's dead."

He said the words so calmly, as though he was talking to someone offering him tools for his Legacy Collection. No screaming out. No outburst. No change of demeanor. The only thing he could say was, "I'm not surprised." And that's the real tragedy, because he was right—it isn't a surprise when someone dies from addiction. In 2014, Matt was one of over 40,000 overdose deaths nationally. Of the 21 million Americans living with addiction, only 10% of them receive treatment, according to the National Institute on Drug Abuse.[2] Nearly 92,000 people in the United States died from drug-involved overdose in 2020, so the problem isn't going away. That's a lot of sadness and a lot of healing that needs to take place.

We drove to the house where Matt was living in silence. The coroner, advising us to remain outside, confirmed Matt's overdose. After that, we drove to the City Mission, where two of Matt's brothers were in rehab, to tell them the heartbreaking news. Then we drove to tell Matt's mom in person. I will never forget her body shuddering in shock and anguish as she collapsed to the floor. I left to give them privacy. Primal screams filled the house. More heartache. More loss. More sadness.

Phil was strong, competent, ready to make decisions, ready for responsibility. Sister Courage was working overtime for him. He held space for everyone during the funeral arrangements and calling hours.

A cold snowy night. Attendance at the calling hours was enormous. Long lines formed outside. People stood for hours to pay their respects. Young people sobbed and hugged and tried to understand the finality of death. Even the funeral director was in awe. In the end, a thousand people

---

[2] National Institute on Drug Abuse https://nida.nih.gov/

attended the calling hours. Matt made a difference. He touched countless lives. And he didn't even know it.

Each person who approached us in the reception line during the viewing shared a story about Matt. Many started to sound the same.

"I dated Matt."

"I'm Matt's girlfriend's mother."

"We loved Matt."

"Matt slept on my couch for a while."

"Matt and I played music together."

"Matt and I worked together."

"Matt and I fixed cars together."

"We rode motorcycles together. He is in our gang."

Even the Salvation Army and City Mission folks who tried supporting Matt in getting sober attended. Phil gave the eulogy in celebration of his firstborn son: the sorrow and pain too deep to acknowledge, at least at that moment in time.

"Good job old man," I could hear Matt saying to Phil, "Love you, Pops."

We'll forever remember Matt's viewing and funeral. He had brought humor, creativity, and love to countless people. Our lives would never be the same without him. A lifetime of grief and healing remained ahead. My grief ran the gamut of emotions.

For better or for worse ... for worse ... for worse.

The words echoed in my head. It couldn't be any worse. *Clear your head, Heidi,* I chided myself. Get yourself together. Your role is to support your grief-stricken Phil. And so, with all my love and strength and courage—and God's grace—I did, and always will.

About a week after Matt's death, everything seemingly stopped. My energy was depleted. The adrenaline ceased. Everyone left. Phil returned to work. Schedules were resumed. The quiet was almost deafening. That spring, we held a ceremony and a formal burial with a beautiful tombstone that had an engraved photo of Matt wearing his favorite authentic Irish cap and holding his guitar. Family came in from out of town. Chairs were set on the cemetery lawn. The minister was ready to begin the service. Suddenly we were startled by a loud, rumbling noise. The roar was deafening. We looked to see what was coming our way. Shock, surprise, smiles, and tears all came at once. "Oh, my goodness. Look, Phil!" I said, "It's a parade of bikers!"

Men and women, one after another, were all pulling up to the gravesite with no end in sight. I could hear Matt clapping. *Oh yes, the boys are all here,* he would have said. Respectful. Beautiful. Sad. Looking into the eyes of several of his dearest friends, I could see the depth of pain and the kindness and love in their hearts. From the cemetery, the bikers formed a line leading the funeral procession parade to a downtown restaurant for pizza and beer. Traffic stopped. These friends loved Matt as Matt loved them. Matt made a difference. Ah! The mystery of life!

Now, when I hear of someone who's experiencing death, I know how important it is to reach out to them. Bring them food. Call and check in with them. At the time of Matt's death, when people asked, "What can I do for you?" I really didn't know what to ask for or what I needed. This was my first experience planning a funeral. All I know is that my friends just showed up. They didn't ask if they could come over. They were present and met us where we were. Only with the passage of time—and in recalling those days of darkness—do we realize how much their kindness gave us strength and impacted our lives forever. For me, *after* the funeral when everyone leaves is when the reality hits and the depression begins. It's overwhelming. The silence. Oh! The silence! So make it a point to let go of your fear of death or being uncomfortable talking about it and be there for those you love. Talk about the person who died; they'll be grateful for your thoughtfulness.

Besides Matt's guitar, we have a small altar by Phil's desk. His photo, his ashes, a candle. We greet him daily. "Hi Matt! We love you." We feel his presence. We miss him deeply. "Please walk with us today," we ask sometimes. We visit the cemetery once a month to plant flowers, put up a Christmas tree wreath, a pumpkin, or put a stone on his tombstone to let him know we visited him. We pray to him, for him. We pray that he's at peace. We pray that he's rocking out in heaven.

It takes courage to walk through grief. It takes courage to show up for those who need you most, even though it's a scary/sad time. And it takes courage to keep being you even when the grief is so horrific that you don't want to be you anymore. I'm thankful that I have my sister Courage to support me through the hard times, push me in the joyful times, and stand by my side as I brave new situations always.

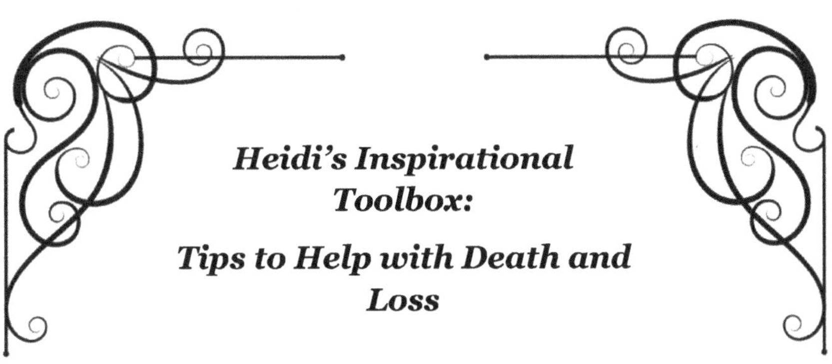

Heidi's Inspirational Toolbox:

Tips to Help with Death and Loss

- When in doubt, just show up. Each person deals with loss and grieving in a different way and in a different time frame.
- Don't be afraid to talk about the person. Share stories from your time with the loved one. The family needs to know that you remember their loved one, and they need to be able to talk about the person's life.
- Continue to check on the family after the funeral has passed. I have learned that the time after the planning is over and people leave is when the pain can hit hard. Learning to live with the loss is a whole new challenge.

The Finale – That's a Wrap!

Who knew that coming back to my hometown would result in me fully realizing who I am? I came home to me. I'm living a real life. Living authentically. Enjoying marriage for 18 years and counting. I'm still learning lessons, but everything we have been through has made us stronger as a couple with our sisters Confidence, Charisma, and Courage and our supporting actors. The City of Angels prepared me for this part of my life, and I'm so proud to call Erie my home. Having opportunities here feeds my soul in a way that I could never experience living in the big city. I have created a tribe of women in this community who support me, and I still manifest my Hollywood life here in Erie via podcast appearances, performing dances and plays, filming videos, and of course networking!

I've experienced the ups and downs of life, including the pain and beauty of living in a blended family. I now get to experience all three of my stepsons sober and living amazing, successful and love-filled lives! To witness how they have transformed their lives is truly a miracle, and I am inspired by them every day. One has a lovely new girlfriend. Two are newly married, and one has a newborn baby. I'm a grandmother! AKA Glam-Ma. I continue to be the leader of my networking group, the Coffee Club Divas. I still sometimes second-guess myself, but I try to find quiet so I can hear my inner voice. I practice my daily disciplines. I say my affirmations. I pray. I struggle with my shyness and often would rather stay in my safe place and stay invisible.

However, I truly believe I was meant for something bigger. And the more I work on my inner self, the deeper I can take my clients, and the more compassionate I can be in all my relationships.

I couldn't to do any of this without Confidence, Charisma, and Courage by my side. They are my sisters. They are my friends. Sometimes I forget to reach out to them, yet when I do, they always appear ... and they will for you, too, as they encourage your creative ideas and enable you to live your best life.

You are not alone. I am here cheering you on, along with all the cast members I have introduced you to in my story. They are here to inspire you and get you out of your comfort zone. It's not so scary getting in touch with your feelings and your feminine power when you have the right tools and friends by your side.

The world needs your story, your light. No matter what your calling is, live it loud and proud. You are important. You are beautiful. Take this as a message that your body, authentic self, and inner wisdom are calling you to play bigger in your life. You now have the support, tools, and tips necessary to be who you were always meant to be. It's time for you to take center stage in your life and SHINE ... and don't forget to put on some red lipstick and high heels!

I'm honored that you took the time to read my story, and I hope to meet you one day, say hello, and hear your story of living a life full of joy and being authentically you.

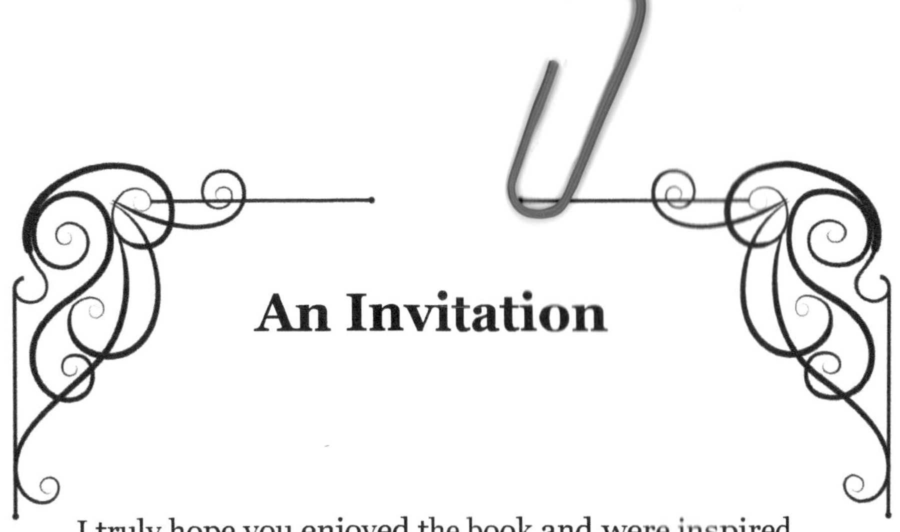

An Invitation

I truly hope you enjoyed the book and were inspired by the three sisters: Confidence, Charisma, and Courage!

Are you curious which sister *you* should adopt?

Which sister you might need to call on more often?

Which sister you can learn more tips and tricks from?

Take my **free quiz** to see which sister you might be missing and to learn how to ask for her help so YOU can play bigger in all areas of your life.

Here's the link. I look forward to seeing you there!

www.HeidiInspired.com/spotlight

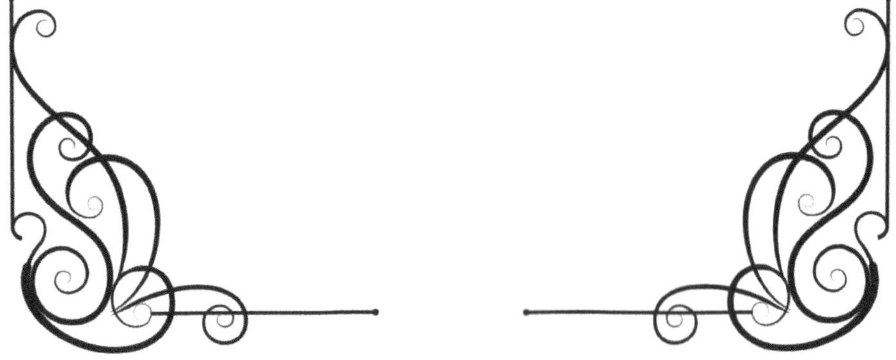

Acknowledgements

First, I want to thank the thousands of women (and men!) who have trusted me in the last 30 years with their hearts and have allowed me to help them step out of their comfort zone to live a little more in the spotlight! I'm also incredibly grateful for the women in this book who gave me permission to tell their stories so I could inspire YOU!

Thank you to Marnie Mead, who was my shining light angel in Erie. She saw the work I was doing with women and gave me a stage through writing to share my knowledge on a larger platform, becoming a monthly contributor to her magazine at the time. She was my first coach in the writing world who believed in my tips and techniques and pushed me to put it in a book format.

Thank you to my developmental editor Brianna Lyle, who took all of my notes which were just bullets and snippets at the time and pushed me to be vulnerable and tell stories about how I arrived at confidence, charisma, and courage. She truly took the book to a whole different level.

I want to thank the amazing team from Aurora Corialis Publishing that has walked me through every step in getting my first book published! Cori Wamsley, the owner, is a wonderful balance between being my cheerleader with so much support, yet also with a keen eye for details! Allison Hrip, the team editor, was a joy to work with! She understood my message and helped me navigate this tedious process with patience. Karen Captline is a creative genius in designing and developing the cover of the book, which went through several transitions. I loved her feedback and learned so much from her. Kelli Komondor's enthusiasm as my PR gal is truly the icing on the cake! Her excitement and energy is contagious. She has created a beautiful media press kit that is polished and professional, and I'm proud to send it to my connections with confidence!

Thank you to all of my busy professional colleagues, and the women who said YES to taking the time out of their busy lives to read this book and give me a sparkling testimony.

And most importantly, I want to acknowledge my astounding and beautiful mother, who is 88 years old. She was my rock as I wrote this book. She pushed me out of my comfort zone. And she utilized her amazing journalistic skills from her past, helping me with word choices and editing. This has been the biggest gift in writing this book: having a beautiful project to work on with my mother, whose love, courage, and devotion have been the strength of my striving.

With appreciation and gratitude and lots of love,

~Heidi

About the Author

Heidi Parr Kerner, M.A. is a speaker, coach and former psychotherapist, networking queen, mastermind host, and founder of Coffee Club Divas.

Heidi has positioned herself as a leader in the arena of women's empowerment, business networking, motivational speaking, sales training, and transformational change. Her coast-to-coast career spans 25 + years and includes roles as a career coach, group facilitator, certified seminar leader, radio host, actress/producer, marketing consultant, author, and keynote speaker.

She provides step-by-step guidance to assist others to get out of their comfort zone so they can live boldly and confidently in their business and personal lives.

Her clients include Fortune 500 companies, small businesses, nonprofits, universities, hospitals, and professional associations. As a seasoned business owner and marketing consultant, she is especially passionate about mentoring women entrepreneurs and professionals.

On a personal note, Heidi is very involved in community theater, the arts, dancing, and performing locally. She loves to travel with her husband, Phil.

Connect with Heidi:

www.heidiinspired.com

LinkedIn profile:
https://www.linkedin.com/in/heidiinspired/

Book: *20 Lives Ignited: How 20 Women Over 60 are Creating Success on Their Own Terms*

CPSIA information can be obtained
at www.ICGtesting.com
Printed in the USA
BVHW012021220523
664675BV00001B/1/J